THE *PATH* TO *PEACE*

A Buddhist Guide to Cultivating Loving-Kindness

AYYA KHEMA

EDITED BY
Leigh Brasington

SHAMBHALA

Shambhala Publications, Inc.
2129 13th Street
Boulder, Colorado 80302
www.shambhala.com

Cover art: Marukopum/Shutterstock
Cover design: Claudine Mansour
Interior design: Kate Huber-Parker

9 8 7 6 5 4 3 2 1

First Edition
Printed in the United States of America

Shambhala Publications makes every effort
to print on acid-free, recycled paper.

Shambhala Publications is distributed worldwide by
Penguin Random House, Inc., and its subsidiaries.

Library of Congress Cataloging-in-Publication Data
Names: Khema, Ayya, author.
Title: The path to peace: a Buddhist guide to cultivating loving-
kindness / Ayya Khema; edited by Leigh Brasington.
Description: First edition. | Boulder, Colorado: Shambhala, [2022] |
Includes bibliographical references.
Identifiers: LCCN 2021054650 | ISBN 9781611809503 (trade paperback)
Subjects: LCSH: Meditation—Buddhism. | Peace of mind—
Religious aspects—Buddhism.
Classification: LCC BQ5612.K445 2022 | DDC 294.3/444—dc23/
eng/20220124
LC record available at https://lccn.loc.gov/2021054650

The

PATH

to

PEACE

May beings all live happily and safe

&

may their hearts rejoice within themselves!

Contents

Part Two METTA MEDITATIONS

Preface

Ven. Ayya Khema was a meditation and Buddha Dhamma teacher in the last half of the twentieth century. She primarily taught in Europe, North America, and Australia. She was well-known for teaching the *jhānas*—the concentration states that the Buddha defined as Right Concentration, the eighth topic on the Eightfold Path—but her actual range of topics covered all of *sīla*, *samādhi*, and *paññā*—morality, concentration, and wisdom—which the Buddha taught in the suttas of the Pali Canon.

She was a dedicated practitioner and teacher of metta and metta meditation. *Metta* is usually translated as "loving-kindness," but she felt "unconditional love" more accurately captured what the Buddha was actually teaching. Metta meditation is both a morality practice and a concentration practice. Ayya Khema strongly recommended that everyone start every formal meditation period by doing at least a bit of metta meditation—always some for oneself and optionally for others as well. Not only does this practice help one learn to love oneself, but it also calms and brightens the mind—both qualities that are essential for accessing the deep concentration states of the jhānas.

In May of 1994, Ayya Khema taught a twenty-four-day meditation retreat near Santa Cruz, California. Toward the end of that retreat, she gave three formal dhamma talks on the fifteen wholesome conditions for creating peacefulness that appear at the beginning of the Metta Sutta—the most well-known of the Buddha's discourses on metta. Those talks have been transcribed and make up the bulk of this book, as part 1.

In almost every retreat Ayya Khema taught, she would speak at length on metta. A transcription of one such talk, given in Santa Fe, New Mexico, in 1992, is also included here, in part 2.

She taught a method of doing formal metta meditation using visualizations rather than phrases. Ten of those guided metta meditations are included as well and represent the balance of part 2.

I hope you find these teachings inspiring and helpful.

Leigh Brasington
Oakland, California

Editor's Note

This is a book of transcribed talks and teachings given at various retreats by the late Ven. Ayya Khema. We have strived to preserve her voice as much as possible here so that her unique style, tone, and wisdom can be shared, just as it was when she was with us, to new and old practitioners alike. You can find the recordings of many of these teachings and more in the resources listed on page 153. We hope you find peace and joy from this profound offering.

Part One

———

PEACE

The Metta Sutta

The Buddha's Words on Loving-Kindness
(Sutta Nipata 1.8)

Translation by Ven. Khantipalo

What should be done by one who's skilled
    in wholesomeness
To gain the state of peacefulness is this:
One must be able, upright, straight and not proud,
Easy to speak to, mild and well content,
Easily satisfied,
And not caught up in too much bustle,
And frugal in one's ways,
With senses calmed, intelligent, not bold,
Not being covetous when with other folk,
Abstaining from the ways that wise ones blame,
And this the thought that one should always hold:
"May beings all live happily and safe
And may their hearts rejoice within themselves.
Whatever there may be with breath of life
Whether they be frail or very strong,
    without exception,

Be they long or short or middle-sized,
Or be they big or small, or thick,
Or visible, or invisible,
Or whether they dwell far or they dwell near,
Those that are here, those seeking to exist,
May beings all rejoice within themselves."
Let no one bring about another's ruin
And not despise in any way or place,
Let them not wish each other any ill
From provocation or from enmity.
Just as a mother at the risk of life
Loves and protects her child, her only child,
So one should cultivate this boundless love
To all that live in the whole universe
Extending from a consciousness sublime
Upwards and downwards and across the world,
Untroubled, free from hate and enmity.
And while one stands and while one walks and sits
Or one lies down still free from drowsiness
One should be intent on this mindfulness
This is divine abiding here they say.
But when one lives quite free from any view,
Is virtuous, with perfect insight won,
And greed for sensual desires expelled,
One surely comes no more to any womb.

The Fifteen Wholesome Conditions for Creating Peacefulness

We can now take a look at the Loving-Kindness Discourse, the one we chant in the mornings on the retreats I teach. Most of the chantings in this tradition are teachings. They are either teachings or they are homage and reverence to Buddha, Dharma, Sangha—either one or the other. This discourse is very beloved, and chanted extensively, particularly in Sri Lanka, but also in Thailand. Most temples and monasteries and nunneries chant it every day. Now, when one chants it every day, one eventually knows it by heart, which is helpful, but also it can become mechanical. They are just sounds in the end, and one doesn't give any real attention to the meaning behind the words. But these are teachings of the Buddha, and it's quite important to have a deeper insight into what he is trying to tell us. This particular discourse is from the Sutta Nipata, which is in the fifth sutta collection in the

Pali Canon and contains some of the oldest material of the whole Pali Canon. So we'll have a look at what he's telling us there, what the teaching is; and when we know that, and take it to heart, it can make a lot of difference.

There's one thing that is of the essence when one knows or listens to the teachings of the Buddha, or for any teaching of that matter which is on a spiritual level. First one hears it, then one might remember it, but then there's another step: How am I going to do this? And if that step doesn't happen, no matter how many discourses one knows or hears, or how many books one has read, nothing shifts. The question is, how am I going to do this? That the Buddha knew all about it is evident. That the sages and the mystics know all about it is evident. But what about me? There's no other way to grow on the spiritual path unless one asks that question and then tries to actually bring it about. That I can do. Then we know immediately that it's a task, and we know that it takes time. But then we also know that one's inner being is changing. And that brings joy to the heart: If when one recalls how in the past, certain things would have upset one, would have made one sad or worried, but having taken the teachings to heart, they don't even touch one. So the question is always, how can I do that? I'm the only one that is in question there. Everybody else will have to do it on their own.

The first sentence in the discourse is "What should be done by one who is skilled in wholesomeness." And that sentence is already interesting because it tells us that wholesomeness, goodness, is a skill and needs to be learned like all other skills. It's not natural to mankind. We have both—we are wholesome and unwholesome, and nobody's exempt except the arahant. So if we have a sort of exaggerated idea of how nice we are, or how friendly, or how immune from nastiness, we should quickly take another look. Or if we have an exaggerated idea of how nasty we are, and how lacking in friendliness, we should also take another look. Everybody's got 50–50. There are some have 60–40. But they're rare. Those who have 60–40 on the negative side usually go to jail. And those who have 60–40 on the positive side, they're even harder to find. It's 50–50 for mankind. And whenever the ego gets touched, in any manner or form, the nasty side erupts.

The only way to gain the skill of wholesomeness, the only possible way, is to know in oneself that this eruption takes place. Now, the eruption may be mild, it may be strong, it doesn't matter. If we don't recognize the eruption, there's nothing we will be able to do. To gain the state of wholesomeness means, of course, wholesome thoughts and emotions. Now when those two are not really recognized to be connected, it becomes very difficult to recognize oneself, how one really is. The thought process is a sense contact, and therefore generates feeling. And if the thought process is a negative one, the feeling will be most unpleasant. And the reaction to that will be extremely negative. And then there'll be a new negativity with a new unpleasant feeling, and the whole thing keeps churning around. So we need to recognize the connection that our thinking has to our emotions, and we need to recognize the connection that our emotions have to our thinking. They are actually constantly in touch with each other. And the more emotions there are, the less clear thinking. Emotions, even those that are desirable, when they become overwhelming, will also create a lack of clarity in the thinking. The highest emotion is equanimity.

So that is why that first aspect of the teaching says, "What should be done by one who is skilled in wholesomeness to gain the state of peacefulness is this." So if there is the skill of wholesomeness, the peacefulness will begin. Peacefulness is the utmost inner level of experience that everybody would like to have, peacefulness which cannot be touched by outer conditions. Peacefulness is also a lack of restlessness; peacefulness is a lack of anxiety; it's a lack of fear; it's a lack of planning for the future and remembering the past because peacefulness is now. And it hinges and depends on wholesomeness. Now, what we've done in the past has no bearing on this moment except for the karmic resultant, and those we have to deal with no matter what. So what we can look at is that we are starting to do now, every single moment.

The past brings karmic resultants, no doubt. But if you remember the story of Angulimala,[*] even with a dreadful past like his, he was still able to change himself and his life completely. Most likely we don't have such a dreadful past as he had. So it's this moment that counts. The rest of the time that we have been alive in this lifetime has, so to say, gone down the drain—it's gone. And there's no need to bring it up into the present. There's nothing we can do about it anymore.

Frankly, it's as if we remember having met a friend. At the time we met that person, we could see and touch that person. We can't do that in our memory. It's not possible to have that kind of reality to it. So we might as well leave it where it is. It has gone down into the whole residue of time. If we were to live in this moment, we would live in the eternal now. And peacefulness can only be experienced now. It's not in the past, it's not in the future: It's an inner feeling, that's all it is; so the future is of no concern and neither is the past. If we regret anything about the past, we won't be peaceful. And if we hope for anything in the future, we won't be peaceful either. So we

[*] Angulimala was a mass murderer whom the Buddha sought and tamed. He became one of the Buddha's monks and eventually became fully enlightened.

can see that even those things which we consider wholesome, like hope for better days, or regret that we've done something wrong, will destroy our peacefulness and are therefore not wholesome. Because this is what we're learning here. That if we really practice the skill of wholesomeness we will gain the state of peacefulness.

It also tells us that the state of peacefulness is something we have to gain, something we have to make happen. It isn't natural to mankind, unfortunately. Most people can keep their anxieties and restlessness in check and are not chasing around constantly, but some people can't even do that. Some people are moving from one place to the next, if not with the body then with the mind, and of course the body is then a manifestation of that. So we have to gain that state—we don't come equipped with it.

If you've ever watched a baby—and most people have in this lifetime, either their own or somebody else's—you can see that the moments of peacefulness are short and rare. Most of the time something is happening—screaming its head off because it's not getting what it wants, or screaming its head off because it's getting what it doesn't want, like a wet diaper or a tummy ache. So peacefulness is very short and usually happens in sleep. Now that's not the kind of peacefulness that is meant here. Because even in sleep there is the unconscious churning away and creating dreams—some of them pleasant, some of them unpleasant. Peacefulness is a state of inner being which is independent of outer conditions, which one creates within oneself through one's ability of wholesomeness, the ability of a loving heart, and the ability to recognize that the world out there is not going to do it for one. One has to do it for oneself.

That moment of recognition, that I've got to do it for myself, is a moment of truth, and while it sounds totally obvious, it comes for most people as quite an insight. I've actually got to do it for myself. Nobody out there that will do it for me. And that goes together with that question: How will I do that?

The Buddha then mentions fifteen conditions which are wholesome, are creating peacefulness within, and lead one to loving-kindness. These fifteen conditions come first, and the loving of others comes afterwards. So obviously, since his teachings are always graduated, and always cause and effect, these are the things that we need to practice.

These are the conditions to practice in order to gain peacefulness, and, with that, to be able to have a loving heart. These conditions are all part and parcel of our makeup. We all have them within us. And all we can attend to is their purification and their growth—like a garden in which flowers and weeds grow, and we need to make a choice. What would I like: Flowers? Or weeds?

Sometimes it's not so easy to distinguish between flowers and weeds. In Australia, a lot of the weeds look like flowers. But some of them are very poisonous. So within our own heart, we need to distinguish between the flowers and the weeds. And if we do that, we can probably remember these conditions and attend to them within ourselves. This attention to ourselves is all that counts.

1

One Should Be Able

The first condition is that one should be able. This means something quite ordinary. One should have ability. One should have learned something. Learning and studying was greatly prized by the Buddha and also by his disciples. And it is as well in our time.

Although there was a time when there seemed to be some confusion about that. Is it really necessary to learn all that stuff and then support the establishment, because the establishment isn't any good? That's totally wrong thinking. We're not learning for that reason, we're learning in order to educate the mind.

Our learning of skills, whether they're on the academic level, or whether they are on the level of tradesmanship, whatever it is, our abilities are a great asset. They are an asset because we can, first of all, make a living for ourselves, and with making a living we can also be generous. We can support others, we can support social endeavors, and we're not a burden to anyone. So in society, the person who has ability is a person who is a great support for that society. We live in that society, like it or not. We are that society. The society consists of people. And we are it. And whatever we bring to it, that either improves that society or it makes a mess of it.

So abilities, on a very ordinary level, are often mentioned by the Buddha. Abilities are also mentioned in the Maha-mangala Sutta, which is equally loved and equally often chanted in the Buddhist countries, and which is the discourse on the great blessings. And there he also talks about abilities—abilities that come from learning skills that we can then also share with others. It's not a cause to be proud of them; it is a necessary aspect of leading a good life. And that's why it actually stands at the apex of the fifteen conditions—because it is strictly concerned with worldly living, and also because it opens the way for a good life.

2

Upright

The next condition is to be upright. "Upright" is a word that we mightn't use very much. To be upright means to be truthful, to be reliable and responsible. To be truthful to others as a matter of course. But to be truthful to oneself about oneself—and that is much more difficult. Most people run around with blinkers on. They can't see beyond the straight horizon, can't see themselves from all sides. It's difficult to see oneself as others see one. It takes mindfulness, bare attention to oneself. And it certainly doesn't mean blaming oneself, criticizing oneself, judging oneself—it means none of that. It means recognition. The formula is "recognition, don't blame, change." Blaming is another negativity. Criticizing is another negativity. And whoever criticizes him- or herself will criticize the people around him [or her]. There's no way we can stop criticizing if we start it somewhere. So that is not the way to go at it.

Truthfulness is a different matter. It's like being a detective about oneself—trying to ascertain what makes one do the things one does, what makes one react in the way one does. Being this inner detective is quite interesting. I love detective stories, and this one is very useful. It's one which can bring great benefit. Of course, as long as our emotions are churning, we'll have difficulty seeing the truth, but we can only do what we can do at the moment.

So uprightness is also being responsible, and reliable, and it concerns a character quality which one can feel in a person. Can one actually relate to a person on a level which is not just superficial? Because an upright person will not backbite, will not gossip about one, will not try to set friends against each other. An upright person is somebody who will be supportive. But also, the Buddha talked about noble friends a lot. So an upright person, if we have such a noble friend, would also be one who might help us to see our own mistakes. This is not an easy thing to do, but sometimes it works. Not always. So uprightness is a character of strength. A person like that is not dependent upon the emotions of others, but has inner strength. And that inner strength can be felt. It creates an island of peace. The inner strength is like a rock on which one can rest in the current that mulls around one in daily life. That inner strength of course comes from practicing—practicing to substitute the unwholesome with the wholesome.

But it also comes from another important aspect: namely, not looking for the appreciation of others but instead appreciating them. It's so simple. And yet, most people hardly ever get near this most ordinary truth. If we would like to be appreciated, all we have to do is appreciate others. Why? Because then we have appreciation in our hearts. And whether someone else then appreciates us makes no difference anymore. And that, all of that—appreciation that we have ourselves, and the recognition that we can be relied upon, that we are responsible, that we are not touched by the emotions of others—all that creates that rocklike quality within.

All of these conditions have as a feature that they are creating peacefulness on a certain level. Now our abilities create peacefulness on a material level. We don't have to worry about whether we're going to be able to eat tomorrow. We're making enough money, which is not unimportant. With being upright, of course, it goes into the inner being, and again, we can see that that would create also a level of peacefulness. It's not the most profound level, and it's not all of it, but it certainly has that level because we don't have any guilt feelings. We don't feel guilty about anything that we have ever done, thought, or said. And should we feel guilty about anything we have ever done, thought, or said, we should try to make amends to the person if that person is available, and if not, make amends to someone who's available. And then drop the whole matter. Because guilt feelings are the opposite of feeling peaceful. We need to recognize them, of course. Some people have no ability for that, or very little. It's a matter of practice, that's all it is—it's a skill. A skill to become an inner detective, that's all. Everybody can learn it. Some people can do it right from the word go. They're very interested in it and very capable of it. And some aren't.

Usually the people who are not so capable of seeing themselves the way they are, are the people who are very covered, or totally immersed in their emotions, or those that are totally immersed in their thought processes. Either way. But as we meditate, we get out of both of those, at least for some time. And so the whole thing becomes so much easier.

3

Straight

The next quality the Buddha mentions is to be straight. Now straight of course is similar to being upright, but it also means to be straightforward. The Buddha was very straightforward. When he thought it was stupid, he said it was stupid. He didn't go around trying to hurt anyone, but he also didn't try to hide behind nice words. He said flattery is also lying. It's got to be straightforward truth.

To be straightforward necessitates knowing oneself. If one doesn't know oneself, the straightforwardness can easily become an insult. That's not what is meant. If one knows oneself, then one is able to speak straightforward from one's own experience. Then it's not insulting but it can be illuminating.

Straightforwardness also eliminates social lies. You know—those little white lies that everyone thinks are necessary in order to get along. They are still lies. If we are getting skilled at this—and gaining skills is what this is all about—we can avoid those lies, and still not insult.

Obviously being insulting has nothing to do with the loving-kindness discourse. But to be straightforward is something that we lack actually in our conversations, and the Buddha spoke about not only noble friends but also noble conversations. We lack it and because we're not quite sure how to be straightforward, we speak on such a superficial level that the conversation cannot be termed noble. It's more likely to be idle chatter, or something similar.

The straightforwardness of one's own truthfulness about oneself generates of course, very often, the same thing in another person, and then we can have a discussion and a conversation which is meaningful. It's meaningful because it also opens up new vistas when there's another person showing their way of dealing with themselves—it may be extremely helpful. But most people don't even want to do that. In their conversation they like to hide behind the politeness of society so that one can't even guess at their difficulties. And yet, we all have the same difficulties. There's no secret about them. It's much more productive if we can actually be straightforward and have a discussion with another person whom we trust. That other person of course also has to be trustworthy and upright. And if that is the case, we ourselves have to be trustworthy too, and then we do have a noble friend and noble conversation.

To be utterly straight means, of course, never to be crooked, because that's its opposite. And never to be crooked does not necessarily mean not to be a crook. It means to have the determination and the ability in one's mind to speak and to think and to act on a level which can never be blamed. Now, that determination may some-times not be sufficient, but that's all right. As long as we know we want to go along this path, we must also have compassion for the times when we lose our footing. It's not uncommon to lose one's footing, but it's OK as long as we get back on the path. Now if we lose our footing completely and slide down the mountain back into the valley, then of course we have to start all over again. But if we just lose our footing once or twice or even three times but always get back on the path we're doing fine.

That's exactly what "gaining a skill" means. When one wants to gain the skill of riding a bicycle, I'm sure you can remember that one falls off several times before one can do that skillfully. So it's even more difficult to gain the skill of wholesomeness and the state of peacefulness. To do so, one needs to have nothing crooked within oneself. Nothing that one needs to hide from anybody. Nothing that we don't want anyone to know about. Nothing that appears to us better to be hidden, even from ourselves. Nothing that could be looked upon as unwholesome. So straight, and not crooked.

4

Not Proud

The next condition is to be not proud. We say pride goes before a fall. That tells it all, actually. People are proud about many absurd things. They're proud about their belongings. Their family status. Their family background, their education. Sometimes they're very proud of their thinking ability. They're smarter than anybody else. Of course they'll have more trouble with the gaining of the skill of peacefulness because they're thinking, but they're proud of that. Others are proud, rightly or wrongly, that they like people, and are always friendly with them. People don't even know they're proud of that. Pride manifests when one says, for instance, I always do this, or I can always do that. If one thinks that, one doesn't have to say it, there's pride in it.

Now pride can take the reverse order. We can be proud of our negativities too. Of course, it's absurd, but people do that. Why do we have that absurd notion to be proud of our negativities? Because it's a support system for this ego delusion. Maybe I'm not great, but I'm terrible, so at least I'm something.

Pride shows itself when we have a notion that we are something special, different, or something that we can put our finger on. None of us are anything that we can put our finger on. We are in total flux, so that's ill placed. But pride is something that people have as an underlying support system. And if we become aware of that, we can, of course, let go. But it is difficult to be aware of it.

There's a story from the Buddha's time about a Brahmin who was called "Pridestiff." That was his nickname. And it's quite an apt nickname because we can say pride makes one stiff. One doesn't like to let go, so one becomes stiff. This chap was known for never prostrating to any spiritual teacher, not even to the Brahminical gods that were so prominent in his culture. And that's why he got that nickname.

So the story says that one day he came to listen to a discourse of the Buddha, and when the discourse was finished, he went and prostrated in front of the Buddha. And the whole assembly was absolutely astounded. They're all watching this; they'd never seen this Brahmin do that. And after Pridestiff, (his real name was never mentioned!) had prostrated, he said to the Buddha that he was most impressed with the discourse and he believed that the Buddha was speaking the truth, but that he had a reputation to uphold, and would the Buddha accept it, if he met him on the street, that instead of prostrating to him and greeting him with reverence, that he would lift his hat. And the Buddha said yes, that would be quite all right. And they remained on that friendly footing. And he retained his nickname. We can see that the stiffness was also something which showed in his body, because he was never able to get down on the ground to prostrate before. It's just that he was so impressed with the Buddha that he finally managed that.

We also say "proud like a peacock." Have you watched a peacock? Well, we do have peacocks in our culture, don't we, and one can see it in their walk, one can see it in their dress and in their whole demeanor. And it's said that peacock—which this may not be an actual fact—but it is said that a peacock is a rebirth of someone who was only concerned with the outer trappings for the body. And now of course he's got it all—he's got the most wonderful beauty, but the most awful voice!

So, we do know that pride is not desirable. We actually have that in our culture, imbedded in those sayings—"pride goes before a fall," "proud as a peacock"—we do know it. But are we aware what goes on within us deep down? To find out is not that easy—it takes meditation. And then when we do find such pride, we can feel that it is most unpleasant, it doesn't feel good.

Therefore it's then obvious we want to get rid of it, no question. As long as we don't know about it, of course, we can live with it. That within our daily life it creates, very often, feelings and reactions which are resentful, disgruntled, restless; but taking it in stride, that's the way one feels. When we get into situations such as a course like this, it becomes so strong and obvious that one does make a resolution to get rid of it. But in daily life, we often are of the opinion that, that's the way it is. Well, it is, but it doesn't have to be. It can change dramatically.

5

Easy to Speak To

The next of the abilities that the Buddha mentions is that one should be easy to speak to. That's a very interesting aspect. Easy to speak to does not mean to speak on a superficial level. Easy to speak to means that one can relate to the person that is talking to one. And relate to the person on a level of equality. Not feeling inferior, and not feeling superior. And that is very often lost in many of our confrontations where there's any hierarchy. Now obviously, hierarchy is not something we desire, but it's there. We even have it in the family. We have it in the workplace, we certainly have it in spiritual teachers, we have it in government—wherever we look there's hierarchy. And because of that, that creates a situation where the lower and the upper don't speak easily with each other.

In fact there are languages, one of them being Sinhala, Sinhalese, where the word endings change depending on whom we're speaking to. If we're speaking to somebody who's higher than we are, the ending is totally different from the ending when we speak to someone who's lower than we are. And that's not the only language—it's the only one that I at least understand a little, so I know that about it, but there are other languages that have the same.

We can say that although in English we do speak the same language to everyone, we also change our wording according to whom we're talking to. And while that often is on a level of politeness, which is fine, it's always up to the one who seems to be higher in the hierarchy to be the one that's easy to speak to.

People who are "people shy," and have no people skills, need to learn that—they also need to learn to be easy to speak to. They must learn to speak easily. Because it's a lack of love that makes them people shy and lacking in people skills. It's fear that the other one might be feeling exactly the same way that they themselves are feeling: namely, aggressive, disliking, angry—whichever way one feels. So one projects. This is one of our worst mistakes, and yet everybody does it. We're projecting from our inner realization of what goes on within us to the next one, to the one who's either in front of us, or possibly to everyone. If I feel like that, well then everybody must feel that. There's no recognition of the fact that one can feel totally different. One doesn't even consider it, because one feels strongly whichever way there is within. So that projection, then, in a person who has dislike, rejection, resentment, makes it very difficult to be easy to speak to.

But "easy to speak to" has another connotation—namely, the connotation of being easily corrected. Not to get irate if somebody does not support and flatter one's ego. That's not so easy. Of course, the one who is doing the correcting hopefully isn't insulting. To be able to take criticism is to be easy to speak to.

In the Buddha's time, he himself tried to show people, those who were his disciples, the right and wrong way, so he did have to criticize. It was not uncommon that he said to Ananda, who was his cousin, and his attendant for twenty-five years, "Do not say that, Ananda." Whenever what Ananda had said was totally wrong. And then, that gave rise to a discourse, to Ananda. Lots of discourses were given to Ananda because Ananda was totally wrong. So usually Ananda would answer, "Would the Lord then please show me the correct way," or something like that, so he was easy to speak to.

This aspect of being easy to speak to is rare. It's something to be learned. And if we learn that skill we will have a very good chance on the spiritual path, because it is due to inner humility. If we have sufficient inner humility to know that, being that we're not enlightened, it's impossible that we know everything, and maybe somebody else knows something that we don't know. If we have that humility, then we are easy to speak to. But without that humility it is very difficult to really follow this pathway, where it makes such a difference in that life, and the quality of life, and the quality of one's inner being, changes completely.

Sometimes the translation of this discourse says "easily corrected." Now we know when we have anything to do with children, there are those that one can correct easily and others that put up a tantrum if they're not supported. And so the parents quite often think twice about scolding because they're sick and tired of tantrums. We aren't so far removed from childhood.

Many people cannot be easily corrected. The ego just can't handle it, just can't stand it. If that's the case, and if that person doesn't learn this particular skill, then the pathway is blocked. If correction and criticism or anything like that cannot be accepted, then there's no way one can progress. Naturally it should go hand in hand with the appreciation of the good parts in the person, but it certainly is a necessary aspect of learning.

Being easy to speak to is gaining that skill where we can let the ego subside long enough and be humble enough so that it will not create a disturbance. All disturbances that exist are created by the ego; there's no other disturbance possible. But the Buddha is particularly talking about this one—that when one is spoken to, one actually takes it in. Now when there is criticism, one should listen to that quietly and peacefully. And then investigate it. Is that criticism well founded? Or does it come out of a viewpoint which does not take all aspects of the situation into consideration? If we find the criticism well founded, we should use it as a learning situation. If we find that it doesn't take everything into consideration, we could then possibly talk to that person once more and see whether one can find mutual agreement.

But if one can't take it at all, one doesn't have a chance either way. "Easy to speak to" makes for peacefulness. We need to see that every one of these conditions which the Buddha puts out are peaceful. If we're easy to speak to, it's a peaceful situation, and it isn't hurtful—it's not resentful.

Every person has an opportunity to have that happen to them, or to be the one that levels criticism. So all of this can be helpful on our pathway which also leads us to the loving heart. Because a loving heart needs peacefulness. It's just not possible to have a loving heart with churning emotions or negative thinking. The two are utterly opposed to one another. So inner peacefulness creates a loving heart.

6

Mild

The next condition is called "mild." Mild, one can say, is the opposite of being aggressive. Aggressiveness does not only show itself in physical actions. That's its last resort. Its first resort is thought, and then speech. And it shows itself very much in wanting to be right. It's an innate and insidious defilement. The thought behind it is, even though one may not be conscious of it, "I'm thinking it, therefore it must be true." I've mentioned this quite a number of times.

If one becomes a meditator—and a meditator is not only somebody who sits on a pillow; a meditator is a person who tries to take within oneself a meditative stance toward everything that goes on—one has seen in meditation that the thoughts which arise are very often nonsense, fantasies and dreams, hopes and memories, and have absolutely no connection to anything that's actually happening. A meditator then takes that understanding within. Unless one does that, one will continue to think,

"That which I am thinking must be right, because I'm thinking it." Now obviously, when it's spelled out like that, the absurdity of it comes to the fore. There's no way one can disregard this absurdity. "I'm thinking it, therefore it must be right." Everybody else is thinking something else. So that would imply everybody else is also right.

Now, this doesn't mean that one thinks continuously that one is wrong. But it means that one questions oneself. What are my motivations? Why am I thinking that? What is it in me that's coming up, trying to assert—to assert its superiority, its knowledge, its braininess; who knows what one wants to assert? Now, these types of assertions make one everything but mild. Mildness comes out first of all in one's thoughts, and if one can have a grasp of the fact that there's far more in the universe than meets the eye, literally speaking, one should start to be a little more humble about it. And aggressiveness will go.

Aggressiveness then changes into questioning. And questioning is legitimate. We should question. We should question what we find within ourselves; we should question what we find in the universe. We should question everything, because the biggest mistake we make is to take things on face value, just as they appear to be. Beneath it, there's quite a different reality, and beneath that, there's yet another one. And so on until we get to the bottom of the whole of creation. And if we haven't got to the bottom of creation, we should continue to question. But we should never assert that the way we're seeing it must be correct. It can't be.

The first discourse in the Digha Nikaya, the long discourses, is called the Brahmajala Sutta, and it means "the discourse on the net of views." It discusses sixty-two views, which are all the views that mankind could possibly have regarding the self, put together under sixty-two headings. And each one is wrong. And why is each one wrong? They are wrong on the absolute level, because each is seen from the standpoint of a personal me. So we should be very careful with our views.

This doesn't mean that we can't have any views. But we should be careful not to assert them. Because there is something else totally different, something more encompassing, elevated, and all embracing, which a person who hasn't got rid of the view of me can't possibly see. So we can have views, we can have opinions. I mean everybody has them, there's no use saying we can't have them. And of course we all think we must—it's a natural phenomenon. But we should be careful trying to assert that our view is right.

Mildness comes in the way we confront creation around us. We could say that being mild is equivalent to harmlessness, which is another way of saying that we don't want to do anything to any creature that we wouldn't like to have done to ourselves. If you ever went to Sunday school, you probably remember that one. We all know those things. We know them backwards and forwards actually. But they haven't had the impact on us, which would make a great deal of difference in our attitude towards ourselves and others.

Now, aggressiveness can also go against oneself—that one doesn't have the kind of care and concern which brings about lack of troubles for mind and body. The more we assert ourselves, the less we'll have peacefulness—because we're always afraid that our assertions, of whatever it may be, will not fall on willing ears. And since this assertion is totally bound up with our ego assumption, it's a frightening situation in that if our assertiveness does not fall on willing ears, obviously, our ego isn't going to be supported. Now when we do this to ourselves, then of course, we have the idea that this is not indulging. But that's also a wrong idea. Not looking after oneself, both mind and body, is a lack of compassion, a lack of compassion for this person who is having all sorts of difficulties. And if we don't look after ourselves, and aren't mild towards ourselves, then it will be difficult to do this with others.

We may have the idea that we can do it for others, but it's just an idea. If we can't be compassionate towards ourselves, the necessary inner reaction and response is lacking. So if the inner reaction and response towards embracing compassion is lacking, we can't do it for any-one. We maybe can do it intellectually, and the more our intellect is roaming around in our head, the better we think we can do it. Unfortunately that doesn't work. It's extremely unpleasant, because again and again we get a reaction from outside of us which shows us quite clearly that we didn't do what we thought we were doing. It's only when the heart speaks that we get the response that the heart of others can give.

I've often compared the conversations that we have in the West with the conversations that I've experienced in Sri Lanka. Now that's not to say that those people are cleverer, or better, or more intelligent. Not at all, nothing like that. But the conversations one has in the West are practically all the time from head to head, unless per-haps when one goes to a meditation course. This is what people are used to. But the conversations I've had in Sri Lanka have been practically all the time from heart to heart, and the difference is enormous. The difference is one where there is a whole atmosphere around one which depicts without any doubt that there is tolerance and acceptance, and no self-assertions to the point where one has to prove anything.

Conversations which need to prove something are happening very often in the West. What is there to prove? Once we can see the reality beyond this one that meets the eye, there's absolutely nothing to prove—nothing. We're all that which we've always been. We will always be what we've always been. We don't have to prove a thing, we don't have to be a thing. Because basically we aren't. We're just a manifestation of creation. And that manifestation is constantly at loggerheads with other manifestations of creation. And very often for the simple reason that it thinks it has to prove something.

It seems one thinks one has to prove one's own being there—being important, being somebody, knowing something, knowing more, knowing less, whatever it is that you'd like to prove. If we would pay more attention to our thought processes—namely, the content of thought, as we hopefully learn through the meditation— one never can be sure what one has learned until one actually practices it—we can become aware of the content of our thought processes and make sure it's mild. We can make quite sure that our thought process isn't trying to prove our own superiority, or own inferiority—not trying to prove a thing. It's just a thought process, which may or may not make oneself and others happy. We need to not believe them to be true, but just to check them out against their wholesomeness or unwholesomeness. Then we would have a handle on this particular aspect that the Buddha mentioned as being mild.

Harmlessness of course is also physical. But there we

already have a better handle on it. We know that we're not to hurt the environment around us, and we also know we're not to hurt the people around us, who belong to that environment, as well as all the rest of the environment. But we still hurt it to some degree, due to the fact that the gross body always has an injuring quality. It is not possible for a body to stay alive without harming something of the environment. But we can be careful to reduce that to the utmost minimum that we are aware of—that's all we can do. Now that awareness of reducing harming the environment to the utmost minimum, that same awareness needs to be within our thought process. What am I trying to prove? What's my intention? Why do I believe that I'm right and somebody else is wrong? What's that all about?

If we can have an inkling of the grand and total picture that the Buddha has painted for us of the whole of universal existence, we have a better chance. If we can't quite see that whole yet, we should be even more careful. To take care, to be careful, is connected to being mindful—mindful of one's own content of thought and one's own emotions. Nothing can be more helpful.

Now if there is any breach of being mild, for a person who has meditated for some time, that person feels an inner hurt. Not because somebody else has done something to them, but because they themselves have done it. If one has not been a meditator for quite some length of time, one still believes one is right, of course. But the more the meditation has taken one inward, the easier it is to feel that there has been a slight breach of creating harmony in the environment. And that's obviously what being mild means—creating harmony in the environment, creating harmony on all levels.

This sounds as if it were something abstract. Well, from a grammatical standpoint, of course it is. But it's something tangible. One can feel harmony quite strongly. One can feel it if one walks into a room where there are some people. One can feel it when one walks into a room where people have gone. One can feel harmony or disharmony. The longer one has meditated, the easier it is to see that, but practically every person who has a bit of awareness can see it. And very often, we don't pay attention. We don't trust our own feelings; we're not used to actually relating to them on that level. But it's very easy for most people to come into a room where there are several people and, without them saying anything, to know whether that togetherness is harmonious or not. It's up to us, to each one who takes the Buddha's teachings seriously, and whoever does that is addressed, to create harmony in our environment.

Creating harmony in our environment is not a difficult task but it needs a lack of self-assertion. Where there is self-assertion there is never harmony. So within that we can see that "mildness" is more than just a word. It's a total way of addressing our own inner reactions and also actions. If we take the Buddha's teachings to heart, we will know that creating harmony around us can only be for the greatest benefit for ourselves, because then we live in harmonious environment.

Obviously we all know what we've done to our natural environment around us, and we know that it is at risk. But we are the species that's most at risk. And this is the species that needs to be attended to the most. It's not just birds and tigers and trees which are at risk, it's us, and not strictly because we have messed up nature around us. We are at risk because we don't live in harmony with each other. We've got a very small planet, and it's full of people. Here in America one does see stretches of land where there are no people. In Europe you don't. There are people everywhere. But it's populated and overpopulated and there are more and more people all the time. So if we don't live in harmony, the risk continues to increase. Each one who meditates can do something about that.

Of course there are people who naturally come to this conclusion even though they might never have meditated a moment in their lives. And then there are those who've been meditating for a fairly long time and never come to that conclusion. But it's easier for meditators to recognize these facts because one becomes more sensitive to oneself, and that's another aspect of mildness—sensitivity, the sensitivity to what is going on around one. Sensitivity does not mean that one constantly has to react, and react in an unpleasant way. People sometimes use that word "sensitivity" in that context. That's not the right way to think of sensitivity. Sensitivity means being more strongly aware. Being more strongly aware of one's feelings and the feelings around one. So for meditators it's easier to become more sensitive, but there are people of course who have always been that way, and have always recognized some or all of these things that I've mentioned.

7

Well Content

The next condition is to be well content. Contentment is one of the aspects which the Buddha mentions as needing to come before meditation. One needs contentment with what one has, not always thinking of what one could get. One could get so many things, yet those things don't bring contentment. If one doesn't believe that, one should one day talk to a very rich person, and find out whether they're contented. They've probably got ten of everything. Contentment's got nothing to do with that, nothing at all.

Contentment is an inner feeling of being at ease with the way things are. Because the way things are, are just worldly conditions and our guest performance on this level is mighty short. And since we're only guests, we should of course leave our surroundings in good order. When we leave a meditation retreat, we are asked to clean up our rooms. We're guests there. We have to leave it in very good order. We don't want anybody to say afterwards, "Oh, these people look at that." Well, what about that guest performance we're giving on this planet?

Not only should we leave it in good order for the next people to move in, but maybe we can even improve it a little. How? By improving ourselves. There's absolutely no other way. If we want to do anything for anyone, we've got to first do it for ourselves. This is such a simple and obvious statement that it escapes people. It escapes them probably in the heat of the idea "I must do something." That's fine, but what can we do?

So we need to be contented with everything that is ours—for example, our body, even if it's sick. It's all right, it doesn't matter; all bodies get sick at one time or another; it's only a matter of time. Sometimes they get well again, and sometimes they don't. So we need to be contented with our surroundings, with the people that we are with, with our own abilities, with our whole way of having a place in this creation.

Contentment doesn't mean that one doesn't learn. We ask of the spiritual path that it will bring spiritual growth. But only contentment makes it possible to use that teaching.

Now contentment should not result in thinking oneself better than others. Contentment should be on the level of humility, that whatever it is that one has, it's enough. It's more than enough, and one can actually offer material goods—give something away to those who have less. That kind of stance brings with it a feeling of harmlessness, because the more of things we amass, the more of them need to be produced. The more that is produced, the more we are harming the environment.

If we are contented with little, it brings about a feeling of reducing self-assertion. It is a very nice way of recognizing that this self that we cherish is really something that is trying to enlarge itself, through all sorts of ways and means. In one instance, it likes to enlarge itself through self-assertion in thought and speech and maybe even in action. And here it likes to assert itself through surrounding itself with more worldly goods.

In our society, it is true that we consider the ones who have more to be more. But this is absurd; anyone who thinks about it for one second will readily agree that it's not possible to be more if one has more. As I've said, we should enquire of those who have more whether they are contented. Sometimes having more brings with it wanting even more. And sometimes it brings utter discontent because of the fact that one can see that despite all the things that one has amassed, none of them have kept their promise.

If one makes do with little, under no circumstances should one be proud of that. We already had that, pride;

not to be proud was one of the conditions mentioned earlier in this sutta. If we start being proud of any of the things we do, again it's self-assertion. The traps are unending! So, there really is nothing else to be done except to make self-enquiry. Self-enquiry: Why, how, when, where, particularly why. Why am I doing it, why am I thinking it? Why am I saying it? Obviously, there will be difficulties in ascertaining why. But if one keeps at it diligently, one will find out.

Everything that one really wants we can get. It's very interesting. If one really wants money, one can get it. There's that much around, if that's where one wants to put one's energy. If we really want the truth, we can get it. It's all over the place. It's within us; we can get at it. It depends what we want. If we make up our minds, this is what I want, it's available. We are limiting ourselves, our potential is infinite—namely, to experience infinity and then knowing that within that infinity nothing and nobody is there. So we have that potential. We have potential for continuous and unabating tranquility and happiness. The potential is there. But it's not by getting anything.

So to be well content has to be now, and not after we have finished the next step on our proposed journey in this lifetime. Now. This moment has to be well content, because then we can go on to the next moment, and recognize that each moment is actually infinity, eternity, as long as we stay with the moment. When we have that as an understanding, some of our craving will reduce itself. It won't disappear, but it will reduce itself.

It may not be craving for worldly goods. Quite a number of people of course have already understood a long time ago that that's not what's going to make them happy, and yet without them they're also not happy. So they may have cravings for totally different things: to have a meaningful job, to have a meaningful meditation, whatever it is that we're craving for. If we're contented with this moment, we are opening up the doors to creating within us so much open space of time and energy, without craving for something else, that with that open space of time and energy, we can actually do something where our inner being is transformed. Transformation is actually the aspect which purification and clarification depicts. We can only be transformed if we first of all agree to the tenet that we want to be transformed. If there's too much pride, or too much self-assertion, we don't want to be transformed, we only want to add on to what we've already got. If we want to add on to what we've already got, there's not a chance of having contentment, peacefulness, and real lovingness. Because that adding on is craving and that makes *dukkha*, and with dukkha, it doesn't work.

Naturally, we always have underlying dukkha. But if we want to meditate, if we want to have peacefulness within in order to meditate and have loving-kindness, to be contented is one of the necessary requirements with which to sit down. It means that there is a humble recognition that the whole of creation is exactly that in which we can find our footing. That we can connect to all of it and we need not be anything special. There used to be a Zen newspaper in Australia; it was called *Nothing Special*. I thought it was a wonderful name. I think they changed the name later; they had something else in mind.

8

Easily Satisfied

The next condition is called "to be easily satisfied." Now, obviously, well content has a connection to being easily satisfied. Easily satisfied concerns worldly affairs. It concerns the things that we touch upon with our senses. If we are looking for refined and better sense contacts it will keep us so busy; it will use up so much time and energy that our contentment will totally escape us. Contentment means to be right there, at this time, so we have to be easily satisfied. The world is as it is. Our sense contacts are as they are. It's what the mind makes out of it.

Maybe at this point it might be important or helpful to reiterate what actually happens when we have sense contacts. Our sense contacts are all from the body: our eyes, our ears, our taste buds, our nose, the body touching—except the thinking—just those five. But the eye cannot describe anything. It's impossible.

Neither can the ear describe anything. Neither can the body describe anything. All they do is have the contact. Now to take hearing as an example, which is the easiest to use, the ear can only hear sounds. That's all. It's the mind that knows it's a truck, or a car, or a bird, or the wind in the trees. And also, depending upon our background and our upbringing, and our whole life situation, whether or not we actually recognize "truck." If we've never heard of a truck before, or never seen a truck—and there are people who have not; very few, but there are some—the word "truck" would not arise. The sound may be called "thunder." It does sound like that. So it's strictly mind made.

So anything that we are trying to get through our senses is supposed to satisfy our mind. Because it's supposed to be pleasant. Now to satisfy our mind through those outer conditions, it's absurd. And yet everybody does it—constantly. It always reminds me of the birds. Have you watched the birds lately? I guess everybody does; they're quite pretty. But they're constantly looking around. They're scared. They're looking for food, and they're scared some other bird is going to attack them; they're scared of the cat, and they're trying to find a niche where they're going to be safe; they're constantly in motion.

When one watches people—and that's a very popular pastime, people watching—one can see that they are constantly in motion. Even if the body might be quiet for a certain length of time, there is constant motion. And that constant motion is the mind trying to get some sort of fulfillment through the senses. It's an absurdity, because the sense contact is momentary, and it has to be renewed constantly in order to bring any satisfaction. And if it's renewed too often it doesn't bring any satisfaction anymore. If one eats too much chocolate, one can't stand it after a while, doesn't want to see it anymore. One's got to stop eating it.

After the war we were given tons of tomato juice by the United Nations Relief and Rehabilitation Association. I couldn't drink tomato juice for years after that. At first of course it was marvelous; one hadn't seen tomato juice for a long time. But if one gets too much of anything it becomes also obnoxious.

So, the senses will never satisfy the mind. And this is something that is so important for every meditator to know: How do our senses operate? And it is a very important aspect of insight into oneself. Check out: How does the sense contact relate to the mind? When we see something, do we become aware? Can I become aware of the feeling that arises through the seeing contact—most people don't—and can I then become aware of the labeling, and can I then become aware of the reaction? Only if I can have the four steps in the mind clear, will I know the preprogrammed situation that we live in.

Then also we will be able to distinguish between mind and body as our first step of insight. Not that they are independent of each other, but they have different functions. The body breathes, and the mind can observe it. It's impossible for the body to observe and the mind to breathe. It's that simple. We have the separate functions, and depend upon each other, and we need to see that there are these two. That will also bring us nearer to understanding our sense contacts, and make it less important to have the pleasant ones.

When we put so much importance on having pleasant sense contacts then of course we're not easily satisfied. Because everybody also has unpleasant sense contacts, and it only depends upon our reactions what we make of them. The unpleasant sense contact creates an unpleasant feeling—automatically. Then we put on a label. Usually having put on the label opens the way to the reaction. ("I don't want that; I think it's awful.") Without the label, it's easier to have non-reaction—if we can see that contentment depends entirely upon being easily satisfied with what is now, and not think of what we have to do tomorrow, next week, next year, ten years from now. But can we be here now? And with that, can we be satisfied with what is in the here and now?

There's no reason and no guarantee that we should get pleasant sense contacts all the time. If we search for them, and if we really want them, we will probably be able to get as many as possible. But is that really a life-time's endeavor? Getting pleasant sense contacts? Is it worth it?

The body can be painful, but the mind can still be peaceful. The sense contact may be totally neutral, no particular pleasure, but the mind can remain peaceful. It doesn't have to constantly alert itself to the sense contact. There is far more in the mind, as far as consciousness goes, than the reaction to our sense contact. We know that through the meditation. The reaction to our sense contacts is the lowest level of happiness that we can possibly get to. The Buddha called it a gross level of happiness. Most of the world, most of mankind, is concerned with that. Obviously, thinking belongs to that level too. And we can make ourselves happy through thinking, by thinking up fantasies and dreams, hopes, or feeling very intelligent and clever with our thinking. All of that can create some happiness, but it is all on the lowest level of happiness. Our mind is capable of much more than that.

Anyone who's sat long enough in meditation has ex-perienced that the mind can do far more than that. So to be easily satisfied concerns our search for sensual gratification. Our search for sensual gratification is one of the three cravings, the first of our five hindrances.* We are, the Buddha said, in debt to our senses. Searching for sensual gratification is one of those hindrances which we have to put aside in order to meditate. But if we put it aside to some extent, smaller or greater extent, in daily living, we find life much easier. Most people find life fairly difficult. But it becomes much easier without that kind of search.

---

* The three cravings are craving for sensual pleasure, craving for existence, and craving for non-existence. The five hindrances are desire for sensual gratification, ill will and hatred, sloth and torpor, restlessness and worry, and skeptical doubt.

9

Not Caught Up in Too Much Bustle

The next one is interesting for most people—not caught up in too much bustle. How many committees do I belong to? How busy am I? Do I think I have no time for meditation because I'm so busy?

When one thinks one has no time for meditation one should immediately consider whether one has time for eating. If one has any time in one's daily activities for eating, keeping the body together, one necessarily needs to have time to keep the mind together. We spend a lot of time on purchasing, preparing, cooking, and eating the food and cleaning up afterwards. Not to speak about having to grow it, which most people aren't concerned with. In former times, one needed to be concerned with that too. So it's not just an hour in the morning and an hour at night, unless we go out and buy a pizza. It's usually a lot of time. And we wouldn't miss it. We've got to eat. Well, by the same token, we've got to meditate.

Hopefully we have recognized that mind and body are two. We are well versed in looking after the body; we've been taught that from the time we were small, when they taught us how to go to the toilet. So we know how to look after the body. Do we know how to look after the mind? Do we know how to make the mind healthy and well, expansive, malleable, flexible, just like a healthy body? Can we do that? Meditation and the inner journey is the only thing that can aid us in this.

If we're caught up in too much bustle, then the thought "I haven't got the time for meditation" arises. It's of course a thought which has no grounding in fact, because for that which is important, one always has time.

Being caught up in too much bustle brings with it a distracted mind. One has to think of too many things. One has to think of the demand of one's job; one has to think of the demands of maybe the piece of land that one likes to keep in order; one has to think of the demands of the people that one sees in the evenings; one has to think of so many different things that the mind cannot really become one pointed in meditation. So if there's too much going on, if one tries to distract oneself too much, it's very important to investigate—why am I doing that? Which dukkha am I trying to get out of today? What's bothering me? It's the only reason for being busy.

There's no need to be busy. One should of course fulfill one's obligations and responsibilities. The Buddha always gave guidelines in that direction. But to be overly busy cannot possibly bring peacefulness. It cannot bring contentment. It cannot bring a heart full of love; it cannot bring a heart that can actually bring the mind to meditation. So one should check one's activities and see which ones are totally unnecessary. And one should see whether, with the activities that one does, one is again not only trying to escape one's own dukkha, but trying to prove something to oneself and others—that one is somebody. The more we try to prove that we are somebody, the less we have a chance to become nobody. And that's what Nirvana is all about. It doesn't sound appealing to some people, because they haven't had enough dukkha yet. When one's had enough dukkha with the somebody, one can actually appreciate the fact that there's only one way to get out of dukkha, and that's being nobody.

If our activities take us anywhere, we want them to take us out of dukkha. If we want them to prove something, who we are or what we are, we will see that not all of them are necessary. Some will be, obviously. It's impossible to live in this body and in this world without having some activity, and one should have some activity. But is all of it necessary from morning to night? Which ones aren't?

Which ones are strictly for those two reasons: getting out of dukkha, and proving I am somebody? And if we find some of those, can we drop them? We then can have more time for the inner journey.

We have the wealth of absolute truth, of immeasurable love and compassion—the whole wealth of the universe within us. It's just waiting to be discovered. But within the hustle and bustle of morning-to-evening activity, we'll never manage to find it. It's like a golden treasure that is lying within us, that we can actually touch upon through the quiet mind. Anyone can do it, but they've got to become quiet. And they've got to stop trying to be something special. Only then can we get at it, and then, having found it, we can share it. That's what the Buddha did. He shared it for forty-five years. With a few thousand people. And today we're sharing it with five hundred million. That's the value of enlightenment.

So we have that treasure. But if we really get busy, we have no way of unlocking that treasure chest. That takes time, and it takes the quiet mind, the contented mind, the satisfied mind. It needs the mind which knows that there is something to be found far beyond any of the worldly enumerations, something far beyond any anything at all that we can ever find in the world. And then we will make an attempt at checking out what is really necessary to do.

Whatever we do out of compassion is well done. And this should be our checkpoint: What am I doing out of compassion, and what am I doing in order to assert that I am really here, and let as many people know about it as possible, and what am I doing in order to get out of my dukkha, to keep busy? But whatever I do out of compassion, that is what we should pursue. Besides, one has responsibilities which need to be also pursued.

10

Frugal in One's Ways

The next one is to be frugal in one's ways. Frugality is considered to be a great virtue. Now frugality is not synonymous with penny-pinching. Frugality means that one is respectful, respectful of the things that others have made or manufactured. It also means that we don't fall into the error that our society has fallen into, a throw-away society.

When I was young, one didn't throw away watches; one went to the watch repair man and had it repaired. And one didn't throw away shoes either. And there weren't any tins, nothing came out of tins. It has taken on momentum, so in the society we live in, things are easily available. Too much of it, all over. Most people can get it when they want it. And because of that, they don't have respect and gratitude for it. Respect and gratitude are two very important qualities in one's heart. And having respect and gratitude, even for owning a watch, very few people ever think of that. They're cheap, they're easily available, all they need is a little battery. And that's got to be thrown away when it's finished. But one hundred years ago, it would have been a major thing to own a watch.

It's not the good old days; people were just as unhappy as we are, no difference. But because there wasn't such a surfeit of material goods, one was more careful of them. And this is the thing that the Buddha advocates. Being careful with the things that have been made, watching over them, and repairing them, and using them to the last possible moment. First of all, one doesn't have to manufacture a new one. And one doesn't have to use time and energy to get a new one. For instance, there's a rule for monks and nuns that when their robes are worn out, they use them for sitting cloths, and when the sitting cloth has worn out, they use it to wipe their feet on, before they come into the hall. Finally, at the end, when it's no longer usable, then one can discard it.

One used to do all those things. I wonder whether anyone can at all remember, turning sheets. It was a thing to do in every household. The middle of the sheet wears much quicker than the outside, because one lies in the middle usually, so it became thin or even had holes in it. So it would be cut in the middle and the sheet would be turned; the outside edges would be sewn together in the middle, and then the thin part was on the outside. Every household used to do that. People have never heard of it. It's just lost. And sheets aren't all that cheap, either.

So there is a certain lack of respect, and a certain lack of attention, to the material goods. Not because one is utterly rich, but because it just hasn't been in the consciousness of our society. And the more the society is one that moves a lot, changes their living quarters a lot, moves from maybe one state to another, the more that happens, the less one is steady in one's place, the more that lack of respect for the material goods around one happens.

Together with that comes the lack of respect for nature around us. The greatest fallacy and the greatest detriment to the earth has been the mental formation, the notion, that it is just something that we can use. We've forgotten that it's alive. There's a lack of respect, a lack of gratitude. Who remembers to be grateful to the dairy farmer when one drinks milk? Nobody. It's just something that's out of the context of our thoughts.

Frugality is a way of attending with mindfulness to everything that one comes into contact with. Obviously, when something is completely broken, one does have to get rid of it, there's no doubt about it; but frugality means to make use of it as long as possible. There is just so much on this planet that we can use. There seems to be an abundance of everything. But there's also an abundance of people, far more than there used to be in the Buddha's time. And they're being added on constantly, every minute. So with that in mind, we can have that kind of inner realization of taking care of things so that someone else will not have any lack of it.

It also means taking care of the things that belong to others as well as one takes care of the things that one believes belong to oneself. Actually, they belong to the universe. There's no owner of anything. So if we have that in mind, we may actually have far more joy. Because gratitude brings joy. If we can see all the things that we are actually using to our own comfort and advantage, that somebody else has made, and are grateful for the situation in which we can have them, then there's joy in the heart. Then a lot of our unreasonable desires, and those that cause grief and hardship—and some of our desires certainly do that—will vanish. Because with gratitude and joy in the heart it's not so important to have desires for other things.

Obviously, our commercial and industrial sector of society wouldn't approve of those sentiments, but then not so many people will ever attend to them. But if we are concerned with our own spiritual growth, gratitude and respect are two factors which need to be embedded in one's heart. These should be easily accessible, especially at times when others don't even see that there's anything to be grateful for. It's quite amazing, how much we can find to be grateful for, and how little we remember that. We remember, for some very odd reason, those things which we don't really appreciate. And we remember them from way back, instead of remembering all the things that are supporting us.

Be grateful. Be grateful for one's health, one's wealth, the efficiency of one's senses—they're all working—the friends one has, the food one eats: —the more we can be grateful and respectful for all those things, the less we have to worry about the things we don't appreciate. Some of them might be from decades ago; some of them might be criticizing oneself. None of that provides inner growth, but gratitude and respect does that.

11

With Senses Calmed

The next condition is an important one: "with senses calmed." Often this is called "guarding the senses." Obviously when we guard our senses, we guard our mind with it. When we calm down our sense desires, it's due to insight, due to insight into the lack of fulfillment that a gratified sense desire will provide. The more we can see that, that gratified sense desires cannot possibly bring inner fulfillment, the less we'll be bothered by them.

Sensual desire is a bother. The Buddha called it "to be in debt." We're owing constantly because it's never getting paid in full. The gratification arises, and ceases, and becomes a memory. And as it becomes a memory and we try to bring it up, it arouses a new desire. And again, the desire arises, the gratification arises, the gratification ceases, it becomes a memory and creates a new desire. Is that any way to live? It can't provide peace, it can't provide happiness, it can't provide anything except agitation.

The mind which has a lot of sensual desire is an agitated mind. Because it's looking for the gratification of that desire. And obviously there are times, such as in a course like this, when the gratification of certain sensual desires is completely impossible, and the mind remains agitated, instead of recognizing the short duration of the gratification, and being grateful for that which one has already, without looking for something else. It's not necessary to have something else. To be contented, to be easily satisfied, to be frugal, these all go in the same direction—toward letting go. Can we just be the way we are and not be trying to get, and to become? Naturally, that goes against our grain. We have the natural tendency to get more, to get another, something different, something we haven't had yet.

Yet there are only a certain number of sensual contacts we can make—we've only got five senses, and thinking. So there's only a certain amount of contacts we can make with the senses; they are quite numerous, but we can go through them in a very short time. We could probably go through all sensual contacts which are possible within a year, probably even within six months, maybe less. And as we do that, and then recognize that there has been some pleasure, the mind immediately conjures up either wanting the same again, or a new one. Until one day one's done it often enough and long enough to recognize that

that's no way to peacefulness. That's no way to become solid within, without fear, without craving, but just being what one is and attending to one's own purification.

Everybody tries the same things over and over again, because everybody has certain tendencies to use their senses. And doing so they find some of it will be gratifying and some of it will not. If one has done it often enough one should finally come to the conclusion that that can't be it. It doesn't mean under any circumstances that we should never have pleasant sensual contact. We get them anyway. It's part and parcel of being a human being. Looking at the trees is pleasant sense contact. Hearing the Dharma should be pleasant sense contact. Meditating should be pleasant for our mind without external sense contact. We have all those inbuilt. We taste pleasant food and hear and see pleasant things. But if we use our mind to grasp for them and crave for them, we're using our mind in the lowest possible denominator that there is.

If there's any refinement within oneself or if one is looking for refinement, then the search for sensual gratification needs to be at least minimized because that is the grossest and lowest form of attaining pleasure. But none of that will stay with one.

The Buddha said about the meditative absorptions (jhānas), "This is a pleasure I will allow myself." And he calls the sensual pleasures gross. Again—they come to us anyway on the human level. They sort of balance out our dukkha. And because they do, we often try to immerse ourselves in the search for sensual gratification, because the last time we had the gratification, it eliminated the dukkha for a moment. But how long is that moment? If one has any kind of understanding of oneself, one needs to check out, how long is the moment of sensual gratification. And how much gratification gives the memory. This is a very easy way to see that there's nothing in it.

The Buddha compared the gratification of the senses with empty villages. He said, there was a traveler who didn't have any provisions: nothing to eat, nothing to drink. Eventually he saw a village in the distance. And he was quite happy to see the village, and thought, well, that's where you'll get some food and drink. But as he got near to the village, he realized it was empty. There wasn't a single inhabitant. In other words, it was a ghost town. So he was quite unhappy about that, but he continued his journey and he saw another village in the distance, and again he was happy to see it, and again it was a ghost town. The Buddha compared sensual gratification and sensual desire with a ghost town: when we're there, it's so quickly over that it hasn't had any real substance, just like an empty village with nobody in it. He often talked about that.

This particular hindrance not only stands at the top of the list of our five hindrances,[*] but it stands also at the top of the list of our mental formations. We want it nice, and we want comfort. We want to have the gratifying sense contact. And because this is so strong, and blocks the spiritual growth with such vehemence, he often mentioned it. It doesn't mean that we can now let go of all our sensual desires. But we should see them for what they are, a dangerous undertaking, something that leads nowhere at all. If we don't do something about it now, we're going to have the desire for sensual gratification on our deathbed. And there it will be very hard to find that gratification, and what's going to happen is that we won't like at all what's happening to us.

So an intelligent surveillance of one's own sensual desires will bring about a far more realized practice of the spiritual path. Because if we let ourselves be disturbed by them, not only in meditation—which of course happens frequently, the more desire, the less meditation—but also in our daily lives, they disrupt our peace in daily life. An intelligent surveillance of those past memories can bring that about and not a hope for something better next time.

Our senses are our senses; they don't change. They're the same. And our mind makes up the story. We need to

[*] The five hindrances are desire for sensual gratification, ill will and hatred, sloth and torpor, restlessness and worry, and skeptical doubt.

remember that too. We are causing the disruption in the mind, not in the senses themselves—the sense base, of eye and ear and nose and taste and body and thought, is not disrupted. It's the mind which is constantly disrupted because the mind has to recognize the contact and react to it. So what we're actually doing is we are hurting, in a way, the greatest jewel that there is—our mind.

"With senses calmed" is such an important point that the Buddha has it in innumerable suttas. Wherever he describes the pathway from the beginning of practice to full enlightenment, this is one step on the path. Without it, we're blocking ourselves. Craving, as we know, leads to dukkha. So all these sensual desires are all producing dukkha in the mind. Then there's the moment of gratification, and then the dukkha arises again, because we want to have it back. This is totally unsatisfactory. People don't take enough time to investigate it. It's sufficient for them to have a momentary satisfaction. And momentary satisfaction is not part of a spiritual path.

12

Intelligent

The next condition is intelligence. Intelligent is a mind that can make connections, that can connect one thing to another and thereby see the significance. If one can connect one's own behavior to the underlying tendencies of hate and greed, one knows what goes on. That's intelligence. Intelligence does not mean that one has a number of degrees; intelligence does not mean that one has read a lot of books; it does not mean that one can do arithmetic quicker than somebody else. It means making the connections: understanding the actions which one does, seeing them for what they are, how do they arise, and what is their meaning.

When we see that connection, then we can see also that if we don't do something about it we will remain connected to our basest instincts. This is what humanity does as a whole—remain connected to their basest instincts. And that's why we have a world as we have it, full of dreadful happenings. War and cruelty, rape and murder, robbery, family disruption, abuse of another, abuse of nature—why? Because we are connected to our basest instincts. We will never be able to disconnect every human being on this planet from his or her basest instinct, but we can at least disconnect ourselves. They're totally unnecessary, we don't need them. A certain intelligence is needed in order to see that connection.

Sometimes the Buddha's teaching has been accused of being elitist, because he did talk about intelligent people a lot. And when the monks and nuns did something entirely wrong, he called them fools. That was about the worst epithet he used for them, but I mean, nobody likes to be called a fool.

It's a native intelligence—it's got nothing to do with one's education. In fact, sometimes the education stands in the way, because one has been possibly brainwashed into a certain mode of thinking, which does no longer apply to the intelligent appraisal of what goes on. An intelligent appraisal brings one to eventually seeing things as they really are. Which is, so to say, the stepping-stone toward the freedom from dukkha. When we see things as they really are, that finally brings us into a different mode of perception of what goes on within us and around us.

The first step is looking at one's own actions and reactions and seeing their cause. It's so simple, really, to see their cause. The only thing is we make excuses, and we justify, and we blame, and we criticize, and we're sorry for ourselves. The last one is a great detriment to our spiritual growth. When we're sorry for ourselves, there's nothing left to do. We're sorry because we feel we're being short-changed, that we're not getting what is our due. How do we know what's our due? Have we got a dues list? We have no idea. We just make it all up.

What we're getting are karmic resultants. And that is our dues list. And there's nothing anybody else can do about it. So, intelligence is highly prized by the Buddha. It's not synonymous with discursive thinking, and also, it's not synonymous with trying to make one's own opinion stick. It's synonymous with making connections: with seeing behind the scene, and sometimes hearing behind the words. But of course, actions are louder than words.

13

Not Bold

And the next one is to be not bold. And that is the equivalent to being mild. The Buddha made a comparison between males and females. He said the females are like a vine that is looking for a strong tree where it can get ahold and wind around this tree in order to stand up. In other words, to look for a support system.

And the male is like a crow, always looking for its own advantage. And of course both need to discard those tendencies. Have you ever watched a crow—how it goes about getting its food? It very successfully gets rid of all the other birds, except when they're too big. But everything else that is around is removed. And it actually can be as bold as walking into your house. There were a lot of crows in Sri Lanka who walked into our kitchen and were bold enough to get up on the work bench and sample the food. I met up with a whole family of crows in Australia that would peck at the window in a huge glass door; they'd peck at that glass door if they didn't get their breakfast in time. And of course, it was a bit dangerous because they have very strong beaks, and the glass door was breakable, so one preferred to give them their breakfast!

This comparison is of course the extreme, and it doesn't necessarily mean a male and a female body. Not at all. It means the male and the female tendencies in us, and we all have both. We usually equate the male tendencies with the logical, analytical mind, and with the will-power to exert oneself and create something, whereas we compare and equate the female part of us with the nourishing, loving, compassionate, and caring side. Obviously all of us have both. But on the other hand we also have both of those tendencies: the boldness, of trying to get what we want, and the tendency to find someone or something that we can lean on because we don't feel competent enough to stand on our own two feet. Preferably they're looking for somebody. And very often on the side of the female it's a male, and very often on the side of the male it's a female. "Very often" is putting it mildly. That's it. That's what we do.

The Buddha of course was teaching independence—independence which brings freedom. As long as we are dependent upon another person—whomever it may be, including a guru—as long as we are dependent on that for our growth and happiness, so long we have absolutely no freedom. Because we have to be attentive to that other person's emotions, and kind of move in the direction so that there isn't a great deal of disharmony. And very often that prevents us from being honest—honest to the other person, honest to ourselves. When we're dependent upon someone else, honesty vanishes. And when honesty vanishes, we can no longer see straight. We know nothing because only honesty makes it possible to see ourselves and the world the way it really is. So this dependence upon other people creates not only lack of freedom, dishonesty in oneself, but also anxiety. Is the other person going to be available? Is the other person going to be agreeable? Is the other person going to be supportive? All those features to look for in another person makes life very uncomfortable. And most people are most uncomfortable.

That's why we're constantly looking for the gratification of our sense desires, because we're so uncomfortable. This inner discomfort creates that search. But we can do much better than that. We can create inner comfort. And then we don't have to look for the gratification of sensual desire. If we realize that it's only our own work and our own way of being that will create inner comfort, then we'll work at that. If we're looking for appreciation, the answer is to appreciate. If we're looking for comfort, the answer is to create comfort within, so, be loving.

All of that, what we're looking for from others, we can create within ourselves and thereby let it come out from us to others, and then there's no anxiety anymore because we don't need to get it, we've got it. It's such a simple formula, such a simple recipe. One wonders why one can't think of it oneself. When we've got it within and give it to others—that's the answer for the search where we think we have to get it from someone else. Naturally, it takes a bit of work. And it takes a bit of remembering, and it takes a bit of being attentive to oneself, paying attention. And it takes a bit of intelligence, but we've got all those possibilities, haven't we? Practically, everybody in the world has it. Most people have some native intelligence, and most people live with that kind of syndrome. It's completely detrimental to our spiritual growth, because we can't make the other person grow, we can only make ourselves grow. And therefore, we need to pay attention to that only.

It can also take on another mode of being: looking for appreciation and looking for the fulfillment of one's wishes from someone else, and not having got it, one may become indifferent, turning oneself away, losing all one's social skills. That's an extreme but it does happen, and sometimes happens with such force that it actually becomes an illness. None of that is useful. Useful is only to foster both sides of our nature, the male and the female within us: the logical, analytical thinking which is intelligence; and the caring, and nourishing, and nurturing and loving side, which is impersonal love and compassion; and balance and harmonize both sides within us.

If there's too much of the logic and intelligence, and none of the heart side developed, it's not only like limping on one leg and not being able to get forward very well, but it's also cold and dry. It doesn't feel at all satisfying and one looks even for more gratification of sensual desire. If one only develops the other side, the heart side, the caring and the loving, and doesn't develop the mental side at all, then one's definitely looking for somebody who's going to do it for one, someone who's going to explain it all.

We can explain everything to ourselves. We *are* that which we're trying to find out. It's all there. So developing both sides within us is essential for a harmonious and balanced life. We do know that we have them, because first of all we can do both, and we also know that the right and left hemisphere are the two sides of us. So there's no reason not to recognize the need to develop both.

The dependency on others, whomever they might be, is a complete bondage, which prevents growth on the spiritual path. We can't be dependent for our happiness on someone else. We can give them happiness. And when we do that, we obviously have it within. So whatever we want from someone else—happiness, appreciation, love, care, concern, all of that, anything that we want—we need to develop it, because obviously it's lacking some-where. And once we've developed it, we've got it. And that's the only way that we'll ever have it. Because if we're looking for it from someone else, it's theirs, not ours.

14

Not Being Covetous When with Other Folk

The next condition is not being covetous when with other folk. That's one way of translation. Another way of translating that is "not being swayed by the emotions of the crowd." I've already mentioned that just now, but not being covetous when with other folk means no envy—not being envious of what others have, or can do, or their looks, or their apparent spiritual proficiency, or their apparent proficiency in other matters, or anything at all that others have. When there's any envy of that, we've lost the understanding that joy with others is actually the only way that we can properly relate to each other.

Joy with others means that we really feel happiness for their achievements. So if somebody sits in meditation for two hours without moving, and the mind says, "Wish I could do that. Can't do that. That person must be way advanced. Don't know how I'll ever get there," then that's the wrong way to look at that. The mind should say, "Isn't that wonderful. He or she is sitting so quietly. Must be really getting concentrated. I'm so glad."

Why is that the only way that we can attend to such a matter? It's not because we're goody-goodies. None of what the Buddha teaches is designed in that direction. That's a dreadful stance. It's because joy is what the mind and the heart needs in order to meditate. If there's no joy, one can't meditate oneself. And joy is what the universe needs. However billions of galaxies there might be, doesn't matter. The universal consciousness needs to be imbued with joy. And if there's joy within us, then joy will obviously come out of us. We keep forgetting that it isn't throwing tin cans and plastic away that pollutes the environment. Our negative emotions and thoughts pollute the environment. And they pollute the environment with such a vengeance that one sometimes can actually feel it, when one comes near a person that has a lot of that.

Joy with others is the third one of the four *brahma-vihāras*,* the divine abidings, the paradise within, the highest emotions. It is a skill that needs to be practiced. It needs intelligence. Practically all of this needs intelligence because it needs the insight to recognize how damaging envy is to oneself. Never mind the one we're

* The four *brahma-vihāras* are loving-kindness, compassion, appreciative joy, and equanimity.

envious of, that person might never find out. But envy damages our own inner being. It's an insidious rust which corrodes within.

Joy with others is something that we can have many times. We may not have something so greatly joyful happening to us, but we may see something joyful in others. So we have a much greater chance of having continuous joy when we look for the good things that happen to others, when we look for their achievements, when we look for their abilities. When we do that, we'll stop criticizing them for the things they can't do, because we will be seeing those things that we can have joy with—their proficiencies, their abilities, their knowledge, their care, their work, so many things that one can praise and appreciate. It all works together when we can praise and appreciate and have joy with another person, then joy increases within us, and joy increases in the universe.

Most people do not disconnect from their baser instincts, and envy is a very common and easily aroused characteristic. Joy with others' near enemy is hypocrisy—little social white lies. Like if somebody has had good fortune, in his work, in his job, in his family, and we feel compelled to congratulate them and within ourselves we think, "I don't know why everything works out for that person all the time. Why don't I have these things happen to me? What have I done wrong?" Well then of course our congratulations is hypocritical. Hypocrisy is an enemy of being able to change from the negative to the positive.

We often justify it because it's the done thing, and we justify it with, "There's no harm in it." There is harm in it for ourselves. The thing to do is, when we feel like "why does it happen to this person and he's always having good luck and I haven't?" is to try to change that way of thinking and feeling, and become happy with somebody else's good fortune. It's very ingrained—one can't always distinguish between the real thing and hypocrisy, because people are able to say one thing and mean another—but it is something which is very ingrained in Buddhist society, to recognize the good things and have joy with them, real inner joy.

When one understands that everything good that happens in the world is also part of oneself, then it's much easier. But when one is still completely self-centered, and self-cherishing, and only concerned with one's own well-being, then one can't see that. But when we see that the world is togetherness of many different phenomena, then it's easy to have joy with others.

One time, Casey, who was an elephant trainer, came to see the Buddha. And he said to him, "I don't have any problem with elephants. I'm very good at training them; I can see exactly what they're going to do. It's quite clear to me. But I have trouble understanding people. Can you help me with that?"

And the Buddha said, "You're quite right. The elephant will have an intention, and he will actually manifest it and do it. But people have a jungle thicket of mental formations. They'll say one thing and do another."

We should not fall into that category. We should be more straightforward, like an elephant. An elephant by the way is the most highly prized animal in all of India and Sri Lanka and Thailand and those countries, and was even more highly prized in the days of the Buddha. It was a royal animal.

15

And Abstain from the Ways That Wise Ones Blame

The last one of the conditions is to abstain from the ways that wise ones blame. And that concerns the five precepts. To abstain from the ways that the wise ones blame means that one does one's best to actually follow the five precepts.

The first precept is to undertake the training to not kill any living beings, but on the opposite side, to train oneself in loving-kindness and compassion.

The second precept is to undertake the training to not take anything that is not given, but to train oneself in generosity. Generosity always stands at the apex of the virtues, and the reason for that is because it is the first way and the easiest way to reduce the self-supportive stand one takes and think of others. It is actually a wonderful way of practice. Not to take what is not given is something that is also very important in business life. People that are in business often use devious means of getting more profit. And if it's devious, one should always abstain from it—not paying one's bills in time, and making far too much profit on goods, and things like that—which if one has any reason to follow precepts, one should avoid like the plague.

The third precept is to undertake the training to abstain from sexual misconduct. Now sexual misconduct must be recognized as being hurtful—physically, mentally, or emotionally—to another. So if there's any misconduct, it also refers to not hurting another person who may have a connection to one. One abstains from any hurt, so that nobody feels in any way upset, or feels cheated in any way. The opposite is reliability and responsibility, and also calming the senses, letting go. That is part and parcel of the opposite, of course. Letting go is seeing that there is danger in too much desire.

The fourth precept is to undertake the training to refrain from wrong speech. Which is, of course, lying, but also idle chatter, gossip, backbiting. The opposite, of course, is the skill of speech. The skill of speech is often misunderstood. It doesn't mean to be an orator, not at all. It doesn't mean flattery, and it doesn't mean saying what the other person wants to hear, and it also doesn't mean that one can get away with just being friendly and polite. Right speech means speaking meaningfully, about meaningful subjects on a meaningful level. When one does that, one feels uplifted. And when one doesn't, it's very tiring. From that one might be able to ascertain what one is doing with one's speech. It's a skill like any other. It's a training like any other.

And the last precept is abstaining from alcohol and drugs. In the original it says "fermented substances." Nowadays we say "alcohol and drugs" because they confuse the mind even more than it is already confused. And the opposite of that is mindfulness: paying attention to oneself. By paying attention, making the connections, we understanding how it comes about, realizing that none of the baser connections are necessary, recognizing that there is happiness and joy and peacefulness waiting within if we discard all those things which are like debris covering up the beauty of heart and mind. When we find that beauty within, that means we have tossed out the debris. We can do that over and over again because there's always new debris coming; it's just like taking out the garbage every week. We don't think that having done it once there isn't any more garbage; we keep on doing it every single week. They come around and pick it up. Well, with this stuff, nobody needs to come and pick it up—we can just toss it out.

And with that, we have finished the fifteen conditions which are essential for gaining the state of wholesomeness and inner peacefulness. And then the sutta says,

"And this is the thought that one should always hold: may beings all live happily and safe and may their hearts rejoice within themselves." This is the thought that one should always hold. How often do we forget. Always. Not sometimes, always. When we always remember that beings should live happily and safe, we will not harm them. And that their hearts should rejoice within themselves, we will do nothing to the contrary. And we wish this for all beings. So this is the thought that one should always hold: may beings all live happily and safe, and may their hearts rejoice within themselves.

Part Two

METTA MEDITATIONS

Unconditional Love
Metta

The four supreme emotions are an essential part of spiritual practice because they are the means to purify our inner reactions. The first one is named *metta* in Pali and is usually translated as "loving-kindness." I'm not that convinced that that's the best translation; it's correct, there's nothing wrong with it, but it doesn't have the impact that the word "love" has, so I'm going to use the word "love" as a translation for *metta*, and try to show you what the word "love" and the emotion of love actually is all about.

It's not what we have been seeing in the movies and on television for these past decades: where "they lived happily ever after" (or not); where it concerns one special person that has appeared by accident, or just fell out of the sky, or whatever kind of fanciful ideas the filmmaker happened to have. That's what has been designated as love, in our society. And people have believed it. They haven't really tried to look behind it. Some people might not have been very fortunate at it—I would say most people haven't—because that isn't what love is all about.

What has been lacking has been a determined effort to see that such fanciful ideas are actually not love at all. The Buddha calls this type of emotion "the near enemy of love." The far enemy of love is hate—anybody can tell you that, and that's not very difficult to understand. But the near enemy of love is attachment. And that's what all this business in our fairy tales is all about. The fairy tales, which most people, at one stage in their lives, would like to make reality. After we find out that the fairy tale does not lend itself to reality, then we have several options. We can become angry; some people do. We can try again; most people do—a third or fourth time. And we can become totally disillusioned and want nothing to do with this kind of emotion because it's only disappointing. We try to close ourselves up so that it doesn't come near us. But underneath all that, there's still that valiant hope: somebody's going to come around and prove it's possible. Well, needless to say, it's all nonsense. And needless to say, it doesn't work. I mean, everybody knows that by now. And yet, underlying that knowing that it isn't working, there's still that little bit of hoping: "Maybe I can do better next time. I've learned all those lessons already." It's a totally wrong approach to the whole thing, and that's why it doesn't work. It's a mistake in thinking, and it's a mistaken viewpoint of our emotional makeup.

So we'll have a look at it and see what the Buddha actually meant when he talked about love. He talked about it on many occasions, and this emotion underlies all his teaching. He was enlightened at the age of thirty-five, which means there was nothing left that he had to do. Yet he taught every single day of his life until he was on his deathbed at the age of eighty. Why? For the simple reason that he had so much love and compassion for the suffering that everybody experiences that he wanted to share his understanding which can alleviate and eliminate all that suffering. So underlying the teaching is always love as the foundation, whether he talked about it or not. We'll have a look at what he actually explained it to be.

Instead of "loving-kindness," we can call it "unconditional love," which is probably a more succinct statement of what it is all about. When we have a look at the kind of emotion that we already have discussed—which is always connected with attachment—we can see quite easily that, if this is really love, we are diminished by it. Because what we're doing is looking at only one, two, three people— and that's the whole extent of love. There are six billion of us, so why diminish ourselves to one, two, or three? Not only that, the whole problem lies in the fact that because it is attachment, we've got to *keep* those one, two, or three in order to experience any kind of love. We are afraid to lose them: to lose them through death, through change of mind, to leaving home, to whatever change happens. And that fear discolors our love to the point where it can no longer be pure, because it is hanging on.

Now fear is always connected to hate. It doesn't mean that we hate those people, those one, two, or three, or four, or five, or how many there happen to be in the house—it means that we hate the idea that we could be losing them. So there's never that kind of open-hearted giving, without any demand behind it that a certain person is also there to receive it. Therefore it's always dependent, and as long as we are dependent, we're not free. This kind of love is doomed from the beginning and we all know that. We can change that kind of attachment to something else, but most people do not have that ability. Some people do, they manage; but it's a rare case.

Actually, love is something entirely different. Just like intelligence is a quality of the mind, so love is a quality of the heart. We don't just have intelligence when we have to solve a difficult mathematical equation; we don't just have intelligence when we have to make logical connections; the mind remains intelligent whether we do that or not. It's the same with love. The loving quality of the heart remains with us whether there's anybody in front of us that we can actually extend that love to or not. That quality of the heart needs to be cultivated.

The intelligence of the mind is cultivated in our society from the time we can understand what our parents are saying. Certainly in all our learning institutions, from kindergarten on upward through university and postgraduate studies, it's always the quality of the mind that is being cultivated. It's highly prized, usually gets paid quite well, and also has a certain possibility for fame and acclaim. Very few if any institutions in the world teach the quality of the heart: love. We've got to learn it by ourselves. Very few people can even demonstrate it, never mind teach it. We don't have kindergarten for it, nor do we have high school, graduate, or postgraduate studies in love. This type of training is not available at any price. And yet, it has made people very famous—but it doesn't pay in the coin of the realm. So that's probably the rub. But once we have seen that materiality and all of the worldly things that we concern ourselves with actually cannot be fulfilling, then it stands to reason that we have to look elsewhere. And this is one of the directions in which we *must* look.

We all have the loving quality within us. There's no doubt about it. Nobody is exempt. But we've done all sorts of things to it. I've mentioned a few already. We were disappointed that the one we picked out didn't love us back, so we decided we're not going love any-body. Or, somebody that we thought was trustworthy betrayed that trust, so we decide we're not going to love. That decision is made in the mind; it's not made in the heart—all decisions are made in the mind. But when that decision is made in the mind, we are able to close up our heart, and when we do that, we're only half alive. Why do that to ourselves? We're making ourselves de-pendent again on the good will and the lovingness of other people. There's only one thing to depend on: upon our own goodness and our own lovingness. We've got enough work to do to get that going, never mind what others do. We're constantly—through our reactions—buying into the actions and thoughts and deeds of other people. What for? There's no need for that; we've got enough to do with ourselves.

By buying into other people's thoughts and speech and actions, we also do not leave enough room for intro-spection. We're too busy looking at what others are doing to us which is totally irrelevant. They can only do it to us if we allow them to do it to us. If we don't allow it, what can they possibly do? If somebody gets angry at us and we feel upset by that, we've allowed that person to enter into our own being. If we see that the anger belongs to the other person, all we need is compassion for that person's anger. That's all that's necessary.

If we really want to know what love is all about, we need to recognize that love is not dependent upon another person being lovable. If we want to find somebody who is totally and utterly lovable, we have to find an arahant, an enlightened person. And since we ourselves are not enlightened, we wouldn't recognize such a person. We can only recognize what we know about ourselves. That's all. When somebody comes into the room who is quite angry—doesn't say anything, is just angry—we recognize that immediately, because we've been angry ourselves. But if somebody comes into the room, doesn't say anything (or might even say something), and is fully enlightened, we wouldn't have a clue. How would we know? They don't wear badges; they don't have any halos or anything. So a fully and totally lovable person is not really within our realm. Are we ourselves totally and completely lovable? So, to look for that is a lost cause, and also it makes life very difficult because we're looking for something outside of ourselves before we are willing to extend love.

To look for people who would like to be loved by us is also silly, because love is the kind of emotion which connects people with each other, and there's no one exempt. Everybody would like to have a loving relationship with another person. But what we're mostly looking for is somebody who loves us, and that's the most absurd thing in the world to do, because that love belongs to the other person. The only reason we like it so much is because it proves something. It proves that we are actually lovable, all indications to the contrary. And since that is the best ego-support we can find, that's what we're looking for. It's totally useless on the spiritual path, and if we're looking for that, we may be disappointed, we may not find anybody. That's the first thing that may happen. We may actually find somebody, but what good will that do us? The love is in the other person's heart. We may deign to return it, of course, but then again we're dependent upon the fact that the other person keeps on loving. And then if the other person decides that they don't want to keep on loving, then all of a sudden that's a tragedy: we're no longer lovable.

That's the whole business of the one-to-one relationship in a nutshell. I mean, we all know that it doesn't work, but why don't we change our approach to the whole matter? Well, the reason for that is of course quite simple. We really need a spiritual genius like the Buddha to show us the way. There are very few people in the world who have that kind of ability to find the way by themselves. There are always some, but very very few. Most of us need to be shown the way.

If we stop looking for somebody to love us, we can immediately turn that around and just start looking for people to love. And since there are so many people everywhere, there's no shortage at all; they're constantly available. Every one of us has constant daily contact with other people. This is our constant daily learning situation. It's not too difficult to have a sort of friendly feeling toward those people that are halfway acceptable. But that's not quite enough if we really want to cultivate this heart quality which then becomes like a safety zone within us. Fear is a human condition, but it's greatly alleviated if we find within us the certitude that we're going to be loving no matter what happens. This is such a basis for safety, where fear is so much diminished, that our whole inner being changes. Every person we meet is a challenge: a challenge to love. But particularly those who are unpleasant are the greatest challenge. If we want to actually work on this cultivation of the heart, this is where we have that opportunity.

Now mind you, it doesn't always work. Obviously. It does work for an arahant. The word "arahant" actually also means a saint, so obviously that's a bit far removed from our daily activities. But we can try, and this is the challenge that we are facing in our daily lives. Those people whom we find difficult, who are obstructing our path, who are against us are the ones for whom we need to find a way to open our hearts and love them in spite of all those difficulties. Now it's obvious that there can come a moment when we are convinced that we can't do it—on the contrary, we're becoming more and more negative. We can give in then, but not by blaming the other person. We can give in and give up and say, "I'm not developed enough. I can't handle this. I've got to try another way." We must try for a long time, but it is not an absolute that we have to make it work with every person. But it is an absolute that we must *try* with every person. Now with those people that are close to us, it sometimes is even more difficult because we know them better, and they're around so much to disturb us. And seeing that we are looking for scapegoats, the nearest one is the obvious one. This makes life very difficult.

There is another way of tackling this: by looking at our own faults and difficulties and realizing that only the ones we have ourselves are the ones we see in another. Our surroundings, our environment, is like a mirror. We wouldn't know what the other person has unless we know it ourselves already. Now there is a possibility that we have actually practiced long enough to have overcome some of those difficulties in ourselves. Then these same ones which we see in another person no longer bother us because we haven't got them anymore. All we need is a bit of compassion that the other person is still working at it (or maybe not working at it). But as long as those traits in another person are very bothersome to us, we can be quite sure we've got them ourselves.

We can be very grateful that we are given this learning opportunity to see ourselves as others see us. It's terribly difficult to see ourselves clearly, because the mirror image is only in other people. But it's very useful to see that, and then use that understanding about the other person, or the things we don't like about the other person, to check out ourselves. "Do I do that too? Do I talk like that? Do I act like that?" We should try to find these same things within. There's no blame involved. If we start blaming ourselves or others for all the things that we do wrong, we'll never stop blaming. It's a totally useless activity, because for any negativity that we have, to heap blame on top of, it means we've then got two negativities. What we would like is to get rid of negativity. So instead of blaming we look at it, accept it, and change it.

The more we have this loving feeling for ourselves of contentment and satisfaction about all our endeavors in our own heart, the easier it is to love others. The love has to come from our heart. So if there is no love for ourselves, no understanding for our own difficulties, how can we love another? We always think we do, but it is the kind of love that demands something. It wants something back. Maybe it doesn't even want love back, but it wants something back. It wants the right kind of attitude from the other person, the right kind of behavior, the right kind of being together—there's some demand being made. As long as we're demanding something—be it ever so subtle—so long our love cannot be pure. Love can only be pure if it's given without any payment. Very often in one-to-one relationships we also have this absurdity of trying to figure out whether the other person loves us as much as we love them. In other words, we put it on a little scale and see whether it evens out, and if ours is a little heavier, we'll take a little bit off so it's even. [Laughter.]

These are the absurdities that human nature is prone to, and it's not necessary because it makes life far more difficult than it has to be. The Buddha said as the first noble truth that there's dukkha. There *is* difficulty. It wasn't meant to be without any difficulty—because dukkha is our best teacher. In fact, it's our only teacher. All other teachers, if you tell them, "I've had enough, I'm going home," they say, "Well, if that's the case, sorry you're leaving, but have a good trip." But if you say that to dukkha, you say, "Look, I've had enough, I'm going home," dukkha says, "That's fine, but I'm coming along." [Laughter.] So it's the one teacher that you can be quite sure of, totally reliable, always there. In our relationships with other people, we experience a lot of dukkha at times. Sometimes they're quite all right, but other times there's a lot of dukkha. And if there has been enough dukkha, we become so accustomed to it that our whole inner being reacts to it and we don't even try anything new anymore. That is, of course, a great mistake—on the spiritual path we do have to try something new. In fact, the spiritual path takes quite a lot of courage because it means chucking the old without knowing what the new one is actually like. If we don't have that courage, we can't go on such a path, because the old stuff needs to be chucked out the window as quickly as possible—or more likely, put in the garbage can.

Our work on the purification of our heart lies in our daily encounters with anyone, particularly human beings. It's not so difficult to love a little bird that has by mistake strayed into our room and we're trying to get him out again, poor little bird, nice little bird. But somebody who has strayed in our room and wants to sit there and talk while we're sleepy, well, there needs to be a little more determination to love that one. It's human beings that we need to work with. All of us have that opportunity constantly, and there's no excuse not to do it, because this is actually what our life is all about. It's an adult education class. We've asked the question already: "What am I supposed to do with my life?" Well, it's very simple: this is an adult education class. That's all life is all about. Now, if we were going to school still, we would have exams, wouldn't we? In school they were usually kind enough to tell us when the exam would be, and they usually also told us what the exam topic was, so we could at least bone up on it and try to learn as much about it as possible. Well, we've got exams in daily life all the time, but nobody tells the date nor the topic, so we've got to be constantly ready. And just as in school, if we don't pass the exams, we are going to be put back and have to do the class over again. Daily life is the same—if we don't pass the exam, we get the whole thing over again. Next time it might be called Mary instead of Pauline, or John instead of Tom—whatever it may be, but it's the same lesson over again. So instead of being unprepared when all these exams come about, the best thing to do is to use our daily lives as an adult education class and see what we can learn from each encounter.

Now in order to do that, we have to practice mindfulness. Without that, nothing happens. Mindfulness is the attention to ourselves that gives us a clue to what's going on within. If we practice it, it will become habitual. Then we will always know what's going on within. And we will always know whether it's helpful or whether it's unwholesome. And we will always be able to change it if necessary.

This is one important aspect of love, but another is to understand that love is the basis, the foundation, for a peaceful life. We always think (if we at all think about it) that peace is the absence of war, that nobody's shooting. Well, obviously that's one kind of peace. But that isn't what we really want. That's not really what we're looking for. What we want is inner peace, and that has nothing to do with a shooting war. They're always shooting somewhere, I'm quite sure. They haven't stopped shooting since the Second World War ended. Recently they were shooting in Yugoslavia, not so far away from my center in Germany. There's always somebody shooting. They might be shooting at us. What is it? It doesn't matter. It's that inner peacefulness that makes all the difference. It's that inner experience that we live in. We don't live in those outer experiences; they're just triggers.

One of the formulas that's important to have and to remember, and maybe hang over your bed or somewhere you can see it is "Don't blame the trigger." Out there, they're all kinds of triggers. What cultivation of this unconditional love means is that within us we have acquired a peaceful zone. We have acquired a zone without pollution. We have acquired a feeling of safety and security, which will be with us no matter what happens. But that's the result; the work toward that goes on day after day, moment after moment.

At the same time, we also need to realize that we only have this one moment. The past is gone, irrevocably gone. We can learn from it. We can see some of the things that we might have done differently, and could do differently now, but that's all. The future is a hope and a prayer. It never exists. When it exists, it's called "the present." Tomorrow never comes; when it comes, it's called "today." And if you have been labeling during your meditations, you will find that a lot of the labels are called "future." It's an escape mechanism. The present isn't nice enough, so I'll do something in the future. It's the same escape mechanism that we have in the movies and the television and the novels—we've got that down to a fine art. But it doesn't help us because that escape mechanism is only momentary. When we've thought of the future and the thought is finished, because it's very impermanent, we've got to start all over again.

If we cultivate the loving quality in our heart (and we all have that quality and we can all cultivate it), then we can be very happily in the present. And when we are happily in the present, then we can also happily meditate, because we can only meditate in the present. We cannot watch a breath that is gone, nor can we watch a breath that's yet to come. We can only watch the breath that is now. Digital clocks are actually a wonderful mechanism to show us how each moment goes by. One little blip and it's gone. And another blip, and another blip. And yet, it's only now that we can live. The future is a thought process and so is the past, but the experience is now, this moment. It's the only experience we will ever have. If we think of the future, we're thinking of it now. So anything that will help us to create an experiential life is of the greatest value. The best experiential life that we can create for ourselves is the loving quality in the heart.

If we find it easy to love others, we also find it easy to have faith and confidence. And finding it easy to have faith and confidence also makes it easy to meditate. If we find it difficult to be loving, then faith and confidence are difficult for us. But on the other hand, if we have a great deal of hate, it's so painful that we know *we've got to do something*. So these are the two sides of the coin. Some people who have more love than others find it easier to fall into the meditative path. But because there is always that which can be loved, and unless one has practiced very long, what one loves, one wants to have—so there is greed attached. And because that promises happiness, people who have a lot of greed often find it difficult to practice. Those people who have a lot of hate in them find it more difficult to fall into the meditation, but because it hurts inside, they are *determined* to do something about it. So each side has its advantage and disadvantage.

The one who has a lot of dislike and resentment and disquiet knows that there is something that can be done, and will, in many cases, practice so diligently that it does really change. That diligent practice has to be connected, though, to the inner understanding, that what happens within—all of our resentments, all of our dislikes, all of our negations, all of our resistances—are just mind-made obstacles. They have no reality to them other than what we give them.

If there's any person in your life whom you don't like or whom you have difficulty with, just put that person in front of your mental eye for a moment. Now just imagine for a moment whether the person sitting next to you has any difficulty with that person. [Laughter.] None whatsoever! Couldn't care less! So it's a mind-made obstacle without any basis in truth. And when we can remember that, we will see that we're only hurting ourselves, we're hurting nobody else. We're making life very difficult for ourselves. The whole world does that. Everybody makes life difficult for him- or herself. There doesn't seem to be any rational answer why we do that. But why do we make life so difficult for ourselves? It seems we constantly want to prove something that's unprovable. Very often we want to prove that we're right. Very often we want to prove that we know better. Sometimes we want to prove that we have real discrimination of who's lovable and who isn't. Why do we want to prove anything? What's there to prove? Don't we just want to be happy? With all that proving, we're never going to be happy, because there's always going to be somebody who's going to disprove it.

So what we can do is remember that the spiritual path means letting go. Letting go of what? Primarily, most importantly, of all views and opinions. The less of those we have within us, the easier it is to practice, the easier it is to meditate, and the easier it is to love. Because if I have views and opinions—and we all have them, of course— about other people, they're most likely going to be on both sides: positive and negative. And then our love cannot be pure.

Love in the heart is the purest quality that we can possibly think of, and it is that which connects us not only to other people, but it connects us to the whole of existence. It connects us to all that is around us: to nature, to the other realms, such as the animals; it connects us to everything in a totality where there is no barrier or bondage. That is the beginning of freedom. Without that, we'll never be free. We have that Statue of Liberty standing in New York, but if we'd really like to be free, the freedom is inside us. We can have it. It's available, but it's work. We've got to work at it, every single day. It's very interesting to work at it while we're in a meditation course, where people like and dislike each other without anybody saying anything. It's a very interesting phenomenon; it happens always. Investigate it in yourself: Can I start loving without any kind of viewpoint or opinion, just feeling that warm connection, that embracing, caring feeling, that feeling of likeness, that feeling of being together in the same boat at the same time? We all share that togetherness—we share so much which we never think about—and if we don't love each other, we're rocking the boat, and is it ever being rocked! We share the same air to breathe. We can't live without that. We share the same earth that we walk on and use to grow our food—even though it gets all mixed up in packages, it's still grown somewhere first. We share the same dukkha of wanting to be somebody, and particularly of wanting to be. We share the same dukkha of decay, disease, and death. We're sharing everything . . . except love.

Saint Teresa of Ávila, who was one of the great mystics of Christianity in the Middle Ages, told her nuns: "Less thinking, more loving." And it's been repeated by so many spiritual leaders. But nobody listens. Yet it's part of the Path; this is why we do the loving-kindness meditation, which is one of the Buddha's methods for spiritual growth. Methodology helps us, but it doesn't do the whole thing. Love is a feeling within us that we can cultivate and develop to where we see ourselves as just being part of everything else that goes on. If I don't love everything else that goes on, obviously I can't love this part either, so what am I doing? I'm living in hate, or in indifference. If I can't love everything else that's going on around me, people and nature and whatever, I'm also lost in this unloving feeling. That's the way most of the people in the world live: lost in an unloving feeling.

Now we deliberately start every loving-kindness meditation with ourselves. Many people find it difficult to love themselves—sometimes because they know themselves too well. [Laughter.] Which means that they're judging. We don't have to judge ourselves; we can just love ourselves. Judging ourselves and loving ourselves do not have to be in the same breath. We can first love this manifestation of universal existence which we call "me." And then, if we really want to make some changes, we can find out what needs to be changed, but we don't have to mix up those two; we don't have to mix up our bad qualities with our love for ourselves. They don't have anything to do with each other. But because we do mix those two things together in ourselves, we do that with everybody else, too. They're quite nice, but . . . they've got all these other qualities which aren't that nice. Or we can see that they're OK, but only if they are just doing something that we're also doing, going along with our ideas. This is totally unnecessary. This is a totally different track—the mind's track, that's where the mind comes into its own. That's when we are discriminating between that which we find useful and helpful, and that which we don't. But the heart has nothing to do with that. The heart just has to love; it doesn't have to discriminate. And when we can see the difference between the usual judgments and just loving—not discriminating—we have taken a very important step.

Another important step is seeing not only that we share everything, but also that our own difficulties need to be treated with compassion. Not with the idea "I should have known better, I could do better, or somebody else has done it to me." Just compassion. Compassion is a very important entry into love. The two are very connected, and they're also interchangeable. The far enemy of compassion, of course, is cruelty, but the near enemy is pity. We're not to be sorry for ourselves or for others. We need to have empathy, not pity. "Com" is "with," "passion" means "feeling"—with feeling. Empathy. Being sorry for ourselves or being sorry for others just aggravates the dukkha, making more dukkha out of it. So compassion for ourselves goes hand in hand with love for ourselves. Some people find it difficult to get at their feelings, not because they haven't got them—

everybody's got them—but because they've put a wall, a barrier, sometimes an iron safe around them. People do this for many different reasons, but mostly because there has been a situation in life which has not worked out the way it should have done. Every situation in life which doesn't work out the way it should have done is nothing but another learning experience.

That's what this adult education class is all about, nothing else. That's what we're here for. That's how we use this precious human rebirth, with all the dukkha it entails, but also all the *sukha*. Sukha is obviously the opposite of dukkha, it's the pleasure. This adult education class is where we can learn to deal with both dukkha and sukha on a totally different level, where we don't have a judgmental attitude. We weren't brought here into this life to be engaged as judge and jury. Nobody gave us that job. It's self-appointed. [Laughter.] And this self-appointment is not even pleasurable—doesn't pay anything in the first place—and it only makes difficulty. But we can drop all this judge and jury business—at least try. In the beginning, one does it a little. It's much easier to love.

Guided Metta Meditations
Metta Phrases
Leigh Brasington

Metta is often practiced by silently repeating several phrases directed initially at oneself, and then successively to a benefactor, a friend, a neutral person, a difficult person, and to all beings. The phrases that Ven. Ayya Khema taught, which more closely follow the teachings from the Buddha found in the suttas, are as follows:

May I be free from enmity.
May I be free from hurtfulness.
May I be free of troubles of mind and body.
May I be able to protect my own happiness.

May you be free from enmity.
May you be free from hurtfulness.
May you be free of troubles of mind and body.
May you be able to protect your happiness.

May all beings be free from enmity.
May all beings be free from hurtfulness.
May all beings be free of troubles of mind and body.
May all beings be able to protect their happiness.

Often today, different phrases are taught, such as

May I/you/all beings be happy.
May I/you/all beings be healthy.
May I/you/all beings be safe.
May I/you/all beings be peaceful.

What's most important is to use phrases that are meaningful to you—and not too complex; simple is better.

But notice how much easier it is to say the original phrases to someone you have great difficulty with—for example, your least favorite politician or a terrorist. It might be quite a challenge to wish that very difficult people be happy, healthy, and safe (maybe you can do the peaceful phrase). But, certainly, you can wish they be free of enmity and hurtfulness. And you certainly can wish that those very difficult people be free of troubles of mind—after all, then they would not be so difficult. And maybe their difficulty stems in part from troubles of the body, so maybe you can do that part as well. And when you understand that the only happiness that can be protected is that which is generated via wise and whole-some actions, you can even wish difficult people have happiness that can be protected.

But the primary way Ayya Khema taught guided metta meditation was via visualizations. What follows in the next chapters are transcripts of some of her metta visualizations. You'll probably want to just read through them initially. But while doing so, notice the ones that you really connect with. Then you can use those as part of your own meditation practice, reading each paragraph and then doing the practice Ayya suggests before moving to the next paragraph. These can also be used as part of a group meditation, with one person reading one of these meditations and giving time between paragraphs for everyone to manifest metta to the people Ayya has suggested.

The Beloved

*Please put the attention on the breath
for a moment.*

Think of a person you love very much. If there isn't such a person, think of an ideal that you adore: something which opens your heart and generates a real feeling of warmth. Having experienced love for a person or an ideal, transfer the same feeling to yourself. Be the giver and the recipient of that love.

Think again of the person or the ideal that you love very much. Let that feeling arise and then reach out with the same feeling to anyone who might be physically nearby you.

Think again of the person or the ideal that you love very much. Let the feeling arise and fill your heart. Then extend the warmth of that feeling to all the people who are near and dear to you.

Let this feeling embrace all your friends. If the strength of the feeling of love has faded, bring your beloved person or ideal to mind and heart again.

Now let the same feeling you have for your beloved person go out to all the people that are part of your life: people you meet on your travels, on the street, in offices, those you work with, those you know, and those you don't know. Let them all be as beloved as your beloved person.

If there's anyone in your life whom you don't like very much or toward whom you're totally indifferent, let that person have the same love as your beloved person. The heart does not discriminate. Only the mind makes those judgments. Let the mind be quiet. Let the heart speak.

Allow the love that you have for your beloved person or ideal to flow out of your heart like a golden stream that has no boundaries, that flood and fill all peoples' hearts with your love. Imagine those who are near are filled with that flood of love, and then further away, gently moving further afield as far as this flood of love will reach.

Look at your beloved person or ideal and be that person or ideal. Become one with it so that the love you feel and the love you're experiencing is all one and the same.

May all beings have love in their hearts.

The Flower Garden

*In order to start, we put the attention on
the breath for just a few moments.*

Imagine that we have a beautiful garden of flowers growing in our hearts with exquisite blooms, lovely fragrance, growing and being cared for through our love and compassion. We can enjoy the garden and all the lovely flowers in it and feel at ease, a sense of well-being, within the flower garden of our hearts.

Now we'll cut a beautiful bouquet of those flowers, the loveliest ones we can find, and "hand it" to someone who is physically nearby us, expressing our love and care through this gift.

Think of our parents, whether they're still alive or not, and make the most beautiful bouquet out of the flowers in our hearts and hand that to them with our love and gratitude and devotion. See the joy that it brings to them.

Now think of those people who are nearest and dearest to us, and for each of them, we will make a beautiful bouquet of flowers from the garden in our heart, nourished by our love, in all different colors with lovely fragrance. Give each of them the gift which comes from our heart and don't expect anything in return.

Now think of all our good friends, relatives, acquaintances, anyone who comes to mind. And for each of them, we'll make a beautiful bouquet of flowers from the garden in our heart, nourished by our love, cared for by compassion, and we give this gift to each one of them, showing them that we care.

Now think of those people whom we meet in our daily lives. People we work with, neighbors, students, teachers, patients, salespeople, postmen, anyone who comes to mind who is part of our lives and whom we meet in our everyday activities Realize that the more flowers we give away, the more soon grow in our hearts. And we can make a beautiful bouquet for each of these people—the loveliest blooms we can find—and we can give them the gift which comes straight from our hearts. Show them our care and concern and togetherness.

Now think of a difficult person in our lives. Or, if we don't have one, then someone that we feel quite indifferent toward, whom we neither dislike nor like, or the one we reject and resist, or who rejects us. Again, we cut a beautiful bouquet of flowers out of the garden of our heart and hand it to that person with love and respect and care. and see the joy that it produces and the relief we feel.

We'll open our heart as wide as possible and extend the flower garden to its largest possible degree, and then allow people to enter and enjoy the beautiful flowers, and each one takes one home with them.

First, we allow any people who are directly in our presence to come into the flower garden of our heart, which is nourished by love and looked after by care and concern. Each one who comes takes one of the beautiful blooms, and a new one grows in its place. And we see the joy that that brings. Then we allow other people who are physically nearby to come and have that beautiful experience: feel loved and given the gift of a flower from our heart. And we think of our hometown and the people we know and the people we have seen there and the people we imagine that are there, or assume that are there, and we let them all come to the garden of our heart. And we see the joy that that brings to them. Each one may have the gift of one of the beautiful blooms.

We might think of all the people we have met anywhere at any time, seen anywhere at any time, or heard about, and let them all enter and take away with them a beautiful flower from the garden of our hearts.

And as we open our heart evermore and the garden becomes larger and larger, we can let all the living beings that we can think of enter, be joyful, and given the gift of a flower out of the garden and feel our togetherness.

And we put the attention back on ourselves as we see that the flower garden in our heart is unimpaired; there are just as many blooms there as there were to start with. Giving them away has certainly not diminished them, and their fragrance and beauty bring joy to our hearts. and we feel a sense of wellbeing, of being surrounded by love.

And now we anchor that flower garden in our hearts so that we have access to it at any time and never lose it.

May people everywhere become aware of the beautiful flowers in their own hearts.

The Golden Light

*Please put the attention on the breath for just a
moment to quiet the mind and become settled.*

We imagine that we have a beautiful white lotus flower
growing in our heart, nourished by the purity of love
and compassion. It opens all its petals until it's fully
open. Out of the center of this beautiful flower comes
a golden stream of light which fills us from head to toe
with warmth, beauty, contentment, and surrounds us
with the feeling of love, of well-being, a feeling of being
protected.

We let the golden stream of light from the center of
our hearts reach out to the person who is most directly
nearby to us and fill them with the warmth and joy that
comes from our hearts. We surround them with love,
providing a sense of well-being and security.

We let the golden stream of light from the center of
our hearts reach out to anyone in our awareness who

is physically nearby with the warmth and joy from our hearts. We surround everyone with love, so that each person feels a sense of well-being, of protection.

Now we think of our parents, whether they're still alive or not, and we let the golden stream of light from the center of our hearts reach out to their hearts, filling them with warmth and joy and gratitude, embracing them with love.

We think of those people who are nearest and dearest to us. We let the golden stream of light from the center of our hearts reach out to them. We fill them from head to toe with the warmth and joy and contentment and surround them with love without expecting the same in return.

We direct our attention to all our good friends. The golden stream of light from the center of our hearts reaches out to them, bringing them our friendship, warmth, care, and love.

Now we think of all the people who are part of our daily life, such as neighbors, colleagues at work, people on our street, in the shops or offices, those we meet on our travels. We make them part of our hearts, part of our lives. We let the golden stream of light from the center of our hearts reach out to all these people and fill them with our warmth, care, and concern, and surround them with our love.

We will think of any person in our life whom we either dislike or are quite indifferent to. Then we let the golden stream of light from the center of our hearts reach out to that person, filling them with our love and concern so that no blockage remains in our own heart.

Now we let the golden stream of light from the center of our hearts reach out to people near and far, taking our love, concern, and care, the warmth from our hearts to as many people as possible. First we touch those who are physically near us, then we go further and further to the cities and towns and villages all over the country, across the oceans, to other lands, and other peoples. We send out a golden stream of light full of love, circling the globe, touching people's hearts as far as the strength of our love will permit.

We pay attention to ourselves now and let the golden stream of light from the center of our hearts fill us from head to toe with warmth and light and joy, surround us with love and contentment, experiencing well-being and happiness.

Now we let the golden stream of light go back inside the lotus flower, which closes its petals. Then we anchor this beautiful flower in our hearts, so that it may become one with it.

May all beings be happy and peaceful.

The Party

*Please put the attention on the breath
for just a few moments.*

Now take a look into your inner household and see whether there are any guests whose names are worry, grief, rejection, doubt, fear. And, if so, ask them politely to leave the house. Because tonight you are going to celebrate with your friends: joy, compassion, and loving-kindness. So show the others out, and let your friends (joy, compassion, and loving-kindness) enter your house.

Fill and surround yourself with these supreme emotions.

Now think of the person who is most directly nearby to you. Invite him or her to join this party to celebrate with you loving-kindness, joy, and compassion.

Now fill and surround anyone in your awareness who is physically nearby with these feelings. Let all of those people share in this celebration. Fill and surround each other with joy, with loving-kindness.

Think of your parents, whether they are alive or not. Show them your gratitude and invite them to this celebration, give them your compassion and let them participate in loving-kindness.

Now think of the people dearest to you, open your heart, invite them to join this celebration. And don't ask anything in return. Share all the loving-kindness you have.

Think of your friends, relatives, relations, your neighbors, people you work with, people you meet every day. And let them all come to this party of celebration of joy, of loving-kindness.

There might be a person whom you do not consider a friend at this moment; thank them for being your teacher who teaches you something about your reactions. Invite them too, to celebrate with you.

Think of the people who are not as fortunate as we are at this moment: people in prisons, in hospitals, people who have to fight in wars. Give them your compassion and fill and surround them with loving-kindness.

Think of the people near and far, people in your same building, people elsewhere in your community and in the cities beyond; invite them all to come and share joy and loving-kindness.

Picture as many people as you can, on this continent, overseas, and make it a huge party. See the joy and the loving-kindness on the faces of all these people.

Now put your attention back on yourself; feel the warmth, the loving-kindness, still surrounding you. Feel it in your heart and keep it there. Keep it so that you can share it.

May all beings have compassion for each other.

The Sun in Your Heart

*In order to start, please put the attention
on the breath for just a few moments.*

Imagine that the sun is shining in your heart. It warms it. It lights it up so that there are no dark corners. Everything is pure and clear and the warmth of the sun in your heart fills you from head to toe with a sense of well-being. and it surrounds you with a feeling of being taken care of, looked after, embraced by the warmth of your heart.

Now let the sun that is shining in your heart reach out and send all its warming rays and its beautiful light to the person who is most directly nearby to you, filling his or her heart with the warmth that comes from your heart.

Now think of your parents, whether they're still alive or not, and let the sun from your heart shine on them. Fill their hearts with the light and the warmth, giving them the greatest gift that you have, letting them feel your togetherness, your care and concern. Just as the warmth of the sun makes plants grow on earth, the warmth of the heart helps to make goodness grow in other people's hearts.

And now we'll think of those people who are closest to us, those we might be living with, and the sun in our heart shines into their hearts, bringing the purity, the warmth, the clarity, the beautiful shining light to them, as our gift without any expectation of a return.

And now think of our good friends, relations, and acquaintances, whoever comes to mind, and the sun's rays from our heart warm them, bring light and love to them, express our togetherness, and we can see that they feel joyful receiving this warmth.

Now think of the people we meet in our everyday life: the neighbors, the people at work, students, teachers, patients, salespeople, postmen, whoever comes to mind. The sun from our heart will shine on anyone and bring love and light to everyone's heart. So we'll go from person to person letting them know that we love and care.

And now think of a difficult person in our life or one that we feel totally indifferent toward. The sun from our heart can do exactly the same—no need to discriminate. We can fill that difficult person with the warmth from our heart, embrace them, and surround them with care and concern.

And we'll open our heart as wide as we can so that the sun in our heart has a chance to go as far as possible with its warming and beautiful rays of light and its nourishing strengths. First we'll let it shine upon all the people who might be directly within our physical presence, giving the gift of our heart to them. And then let that sun from your heart reach out to all the people who you know are somewhat nearby: those you've seen, those you've not seen, those you have to assume are there. The sun is capable of making love grow. The more strength it has, the more warmth others will feel.

And now we'll let the sun from our heart shine on the people who live in our community. We may not know them, but we know they're there. The sun doesn't know us, but it shines on us and makes flowers and food and trees and bushes grow. So too will the sun from our heart make love grow.

And then we go further, as far as the strength of our heart will reach. Let the sun shine on people in towns and villages and cities near and far all over the country, in the surrounding countries, across the oceans, and in your hometown. Let the sun from your heart bring warmth and love to the people that you know or can think of, have heard about or seen, or just assume to be there.

And now let the sun from our hearts shine on all that surrounds us: trees, meadows, valleys, mountains, flowers, bushes, grass, the sky, the clouds, sun, moon, stars. The sun from our heart has beautiful warmth and rays and can embrace it all.

And we'll put the attention back on ourselves and feel the buoyancy and the lightness which comes from the purity of the heart. We feel the joy that comes from loving and giving our love. And we enter into our heart, seeing it lit up, nourished by the warmth of love, clear, with nothing hidden, and feel totally secure in that.

May people everywhere become aware of the sun in their hearts.

The Fountain of Love

*Please put the attention on the breath
for just a moment.*

Imagine that you have a fountain in your heart, a fountain of love. The water of this fountain as it keeps bubbling up and spreading, and has its beautiful appearance—all of that is filled with love. Every drop of water that comes out of that fountain is a drop of love.

So let yourself be filled by that fountain of love from head to toe.

Now imagine that you are standing under this fountain and these drops of love cover you completely.

Now let this fountain become powerful enough so that its drops of love can fall into the heart of the person nearest to you. Let it be a beautiful fountain in movement and appearance. So powerful that the drops can go right into your neighbor's heart.

Make the fountain so large that everyone who might be physically nearby can stand under it and be drenched with love. The drops that come out of this fountain bring joy to everyone. But the source of the fountain remains in your heart.

Now let this fountain that comes out of your heart use its beautiful drops to fill your parents' hearts. They, too, are part of the beauty and refreshment that comes from this fountain of love.

Let this fountain reach out to those nearest and dearest to you. Let them be filled and refreshed, each drop containing love.

All your good friends will now partake of this fountain of love. Make it embracing enough, so that they can all partake in the refreshment and beauty of it.

Now let the force of the fountain in your heart be strong enough so that all the people who are part of your life can receive the drops of love that rain down from it.

If there is anyone whom you do not like, do not love, take that person into your heart so that the fountain of love can refresh and renew the joy in that person's heart also.

Put so much love in that fountain that its spray becomes larger and larger and more encompassing. Give it more and more power so that it can reach far and wide. First it reaches the people who are near, then further and further afield. Make that fountain bigger and bigger, more and more powerful. Put more and more love into it to give it energy, give it strength to reach ever further. Let these drops of love fall down into the hearts of beings as far as the strength of this fountain will reach.

Now put your attention back on yourself. Let this fountain of love remain in your heart to refresh and to strengthen you. Continue to let the drops of love fill you and surround you, always available, always the source of joy for yourself and others. Let the fountain remain part of your heart.

May all beings have love in their hearts.

Breathe In Peace,
Breathe Out Love

Please put the attention on the breath
for just a few moments.

With each breath that you take, imagine that you are breathing into yourself peacefulness. Wherever you think you can get it from, breathe it into yourself— maybe from the night sky with the stars, maybe from the trees around us, maybe from the stillness in the air, or the mountains in the distance, or just from your breath. Breathe it into yourself. Let it settle within. Let it fill you. And on your out-breath, think that you are breathing out love from your heart—the warm embracing acceptance and care. And let that warm embrace of love that you are breathing out surround you in an embrace.

Now breathe out that love and peace that is within you. Breathe it out to the person next to you. Give it as your gift. Through breath that is life and that connects us all. Because we are breathing the same air.

And now breathe that love and peace within you out to everyone here. Let everyone be part of your breath containing love and peace. Fill everyone and embrace everyone.

Now breathe love and peace out to your parents. They too are connected through breath, through air. No discrimination is needed. We are all just part of the whole. And let that part of you that is love and peace come out and fill your parents and embrace them.

Now breathe out love and peace to your nearest and dearest people. You have breath. You have love. And you have peace. Share it. No other reason. The more we give, the more we have.

Now breathe out love and peace to all your friends. Let them arise before your mind's eye. Let each one share what you have.

Think of the people you know, whom you meet in your daily life. Breathe love and peace out to them. Embrace them with the warmth of your care and acceptance and fill them with peacefulness. Share what you have. Think of all the people you meet in your daily life.

Think of anyone you don't like or, if there is no such person, anyone to whom you are quite indifferent, who means nothing to you. And breathe out love and peace to that person. They share the same air, the same earth.

And now let your breath carry love and peace to as many people you can possibly think of. In your building, in your community, wherever you think that people can be found. In the houses. On the street. And further afield. Think of people wherever they may be. Let your breath carry your love and your peace to each one of them. Letting them share in the best that we can give them. And further afield, as far as the strength and the power of your love and your peacefulness will reach.

And put your attention back onto yourself. Breathe in peace with each in-breath and fill yourself with peacefulness. Breathe out love with each out-breath; breathe out love and acceptance and care. And the lovely feeling of being totally protected. Do this with each in and out-breath.

May all beings have love and peace in their hearts.

Forgiveness

Please put the attention on the breath.

Have forgiveness in your heart for anything you think you've done wrong. Forgive yourself for all the past omissions and commissions. They are long gone. Understand that you were a different person then and this one is forgiving the one that you were. Feel that forgiveness filling you and enveloping you with a sense of warmth and ease.

Think of your parents. Forgive them for anything you have ever blamed them for. Understand that they too are different now. Let this forgiveness fill them, surround them, knowing in your heart that this is your most wonderful way of togetherness.

Think of your nearest and dearest people. Forgive them for anything that you think they have done wrong or are doing wrong at this time. Fill them with your forgiveness. Let them feel that you accept them. Let that forgiveness fill them, realizing that this is your expression of love.

Now think of your friends. Forgive them for anything you have disliked about them. Let your forgiveness reach out to them, so that they can be filled with it, embraced by it.

Think of the people you know, whomever they might be, and forgive them all for whatever it is that you have blamed them for, that you have judged them for, that you have disliked. Let your forgiveness fill their hearts, surround them, envelope them, be your expression of love for them.

Now think of any special person whom you really need to forgive. Toward whom you still have resentment, rejection, dislike. Forgive him or her fully. Remember that everyone has dukkha. Let this forgiveness come from your heart. Reach out to that person, complete and total.

Think of any one person, or any situation, or any group of people whom you are condemning, blaming, disliking. Forgive them, completely. Let your forgiveness be your expression of unconditional love. They may not do the right things. Human beings have dukkha. And your heart needs the forgiveness in order to have purity of love.

Have a look again and see whether there's anyone or anything, anywhere in the world, toward whom you have blame or condemnation. And forgive the people or the person, so that there is no separation in your heart.

Now put your attention back on yourself. And recognize the goodness in you. The effort you are making. Feel the warmth and ease that comes from forgiveness.

May all beings have forgiveness in their hearts.

The Goodness of Yourself and Others

*Please put the attention on the breath
for just a few moments.*

Think of all the nice things you have ever done in your life, such as helping another person, being concerned about another's welfare, being loving and kind, giving a present—anything that you can think of that you think was a good thought or deed.

Remember them now. And then feel warm and loving toward yourself, recognizing all the goodness in yourself.

Think of the people who are close to you. Think of all the good deeds that they have ever done. Good deeds that you know of and those that you assume. Appreciate these people and love them because of the goodness you can feel in them.

Think of the people you know. Let them arise before your mind's eye. And think of all their good deeds that you know about or that you surmise in them. Feel your heart going out to them. Appreciating . . . loving . . . respecting . . . the goodness in them.

Think of those people who are part of your life but toward whom you feel quite indifferent. You meet them here and there. You don't have any real connection to them. Think of all the good things they have done . . . possibly for you. Appreciate and love them and respect them. Make your heart reach out to them.

Now think of anyone you don't like or who is bothering you in any way. And then think of all the good things that person has ever thought, said, or done. Whether you were actually present or not. Appreciate and respect that person for his or her goodness. Let your heart go out to him or her. Feel the sameness, the oneness, that unites all of us.

Think of people in your hometown. Those you know and those you don't know. Remember all the good things you know about them, imagine the others, appreciate them, let your heart reach out and connect with their hearts.

Now think of people everywhere. In the towns, in the cities, in the villages, on the land. All of them looking for happiness. All of them having goodness in their hearts. Connect with that goodness, connect with their hearts. Let your appreciation, your warmth and respect, for all these beings, flow out of your heart and help to lift the consciousness that is present in humanity.

Now put your attention back onto yourself. And feel the ease that comes when consciousness goes to goodness and lovingness. Feel how the mind feels lighter, pleased, carefree, and the heart feels loving. Connect with the goodness in yourself. See it clearly. Anchor that recognition within your heart, so you can retain it. Never lose sight of it. And feel the appreciation and warmth welling up within you, connected to that goodness.

May beings everywhere appreciate and respect each other.

The Seed of Enlightenment

*In order to start, please put the attention
on the breath for just a few moments.*

Look into your heart and see that there is a shining jewel
in there, beautiful, translucent, giving off many colors—
the most valuable thing that one can find in the universe,
the seed of enlightenment. Look at it. It soothes your
heart and you can love yourself because you carry that
within. And the love that you feel is the nourishment for
that seed to develop. In the warmth of your heart, give
that beautiful seed within the necessary ground that it
needs to grow. And you can be joyful at seeing that this
wonderful jewel exists in your heart.

Now put your attention on the person who might be
most physically nearby to you and notice that the same
jewel, translucent, shining, reflecting many colors of the
greatest value, lives in that person's heart. And you can

fill that person from head to toe with the warmth of love—it's the only thing that you can do to help to make that seed into a beautiful flower.

And think of your parents, whether they're still alive or not, and see that beautiful seed of enlightenment in their hearts—the most valuable jewel there is in this world and in the whole of the universe. And you can love them and care for them as the carriers of this beauty.

And now think of those people who are nearest and dearest to us that we might be living with, and each one carries that same jewel, the seed of enlightenment within, which illuminates the whole heart when we allow it to do so. And our love and compassion and care and concern can fill the hearts of these people, giving nourishment so that the seed can grow.

And we think of our friends, acquaintances, relatives, anyone that comes to mind, anyone at all that we would like to extend the warmth of our love and the care of our compassion to. We look into their hearts and see exactly what we have in our own, the jewel of the seed of enlightenment, and we can love them and embrace them and manifest our togetherness that way.

Think of all the people whom we meet in our everyday life, whoever they might be, whoever comes to mind—our neighbors, people at work, people in the shops, in the offices, on the road, in the cars, whomever it is we meet, whom we might talk to or just see. All of them carry that same beautiful jewel, the seed of enlightenment within. It is easy to love them, to care for them, to manifest our togetherness because we know they have that which is of the greatest value, the same as we do. So we extend the warmth of our hearts to them and manifest the togetherness that we feel and the care and help that our love can give them.

And now think of a difficult person, anyone whom we have been angry at, have rejected, or anyone who has been angry at us or has rejected us. Each one carries the same jewel, the seed of enlightenment within, in their hearts, and only love is the nourishment that can make that seed grow and develop and become a beautiful flower. And again we realize the togetherness with that person, the sameness, the non-separation, and the warmth of our heart extends also to the difficult people.

And now take a look at people everywhere, whatever comes to mind. Those who are nearby—all the people in the surrounding houses, people in the towns, cities, on the land, all over the country; there isn't one who doesn't have that same jewel in their heart. And it's easy to love these people, to feel connected, to manifest the warmth and embrace and to know that that's the only way they can live together in peace and develop the seed of enlightenment. Wherever we look, each heart has it—it's of the greatest beauty and magnificent value. And so our love can flow easily, everywhere, unimpeded.

And we put our attention back on ourselves and take a look into our heart. Can we see that this wonderful jewel that we carry within has become a little more shiny, is reflecting magnificent colors and takes pride of place in our hearts? And since we can love that jewel, we can fill ourselves from head to toe with the warmth of love and surround ourselves with the care of compassion and feel at ease and protected.

May people everywhere cultivate the seed of enlightenment in their own heart.

Afterword

I used the word "universal" a couple of times earlier, and now I want to share something with you:

Our star, the sun, is one of several hundred billion—hundred billion—stars in the Milky Way galaxy. The star closest to our sun is 4.5 light years away. A light year is the distance light travels in one year. Light moves at 186,272 miles per second. Our sun is 30,000 light years from the center of the Milky Way. So the light you see coming from our galaxy center left there 30,000 years ago. The universe contains at least a hundred billion other galaxies. Each galaxy contains at least a hundred billion stars.

The reason I'm sharing this is to put into context the size of our problems. When you compare our problems to the scale of the universe, they seem so minute that we might wonder, *Why?* and *What is our worry for?* At night, from much of the world, you can see the Milky Way quite easily if it's dark enough. From where we stand, it looks small, everything is like a pin point. But imagine what our existence looks like from up there, looking down at us—even smaller. So if we keep this sort of thing in mind, and recognize the immensity of creation, we may be able to have a perspective that is less self-oriented, and more universal. And when that happens, things just fall into place far more easily. We won't have to worry about our own desires so much—whether they come true or not—and we won't worry about our own importance. What we can attend to is our own growth, and when we do, the universe gains positivity. How much? Who knows. It may be minutely, but it is better that it minutely gains, than that it minutely loses.

The Buddha said that one can't stand still; it's impossible. There's nothing that stands still in a person; one either grows or retards. We either grow in our understanding and purity, or we're going backwards. So, maybe in the context of the size of this universe, we might see this as a personal goal.

Acknowledgments

This book came to be because Diana Gould asked me a question: If she transcribed the three one-and-a-quarter-hour dhamma talks Ayya Khema gave on the fifteen qualities mentioned at the beginning of the Metta Sutta, would I edit the transcriptions into a book? She transcribed them and the talks are now part 1 of this volume. The dhamma talk from Santa Fe at the beginning of part 2, "Unconditional Love: Metta," was transcribed by Brian Kelley. The guided metta meditations in part 2 were transcribed by Brad Bettinger. These three people made this book possible—but only thanks equally to Ven. Ayya Khema and her brilliant teaching, of course.

Bibliography

Bodhi, Bhikkhu, trans. *Connected Discourses of the Buddha: A Translation of the Saṃyutta Nikāya.* Somerville, MA: Wisdom Publications, 2003.

—————, trans. *The Numerical Discourses of the Buddha: A Translation of the Aṅguttara Nikāya.* Somerville, MA: Wisdom Publications, 2012.

Ireland, John D., trans. *The Udāna and the Itivuttaka.* Kandy, Sri Lanka: Buddhist Publication Society, 1998

Ñanamoli, Bhikkhu, and Bhikkhu Bodhi, trans. *The Middle Length Discourses of the Buddha: A Translation of the Majjhima Nikāya.* Somerville, MA: Wisdom Publications, 1995.

Norman, K. R., trans. *The Rhinoceros Horn and Other Early Buddhist Poems (Sutta Nipāta).* Oxford: Pali Text Society, 1996.

Walshe, Maurice, trans. *The Long Discourses of the Buddha: A Translation of the Dīgha Nikāya.* Somerville, MA: Wisdom Publications, 1995.

Resources

Audio for the source material on which this book is based is available through the Dharma Seed organization, as indicated for each entry below.

The chapters on the Fifteen Wholesome Conditions for Creating Peacefulness in part 1 were transcribed from the following talks:

Khema, Ayya. "The Discourse on Loving-Kindness (*Karaniya Metta Sutta*)." Recorded June 4, 1994. http://dharmaseed.org/teacher/334/talk/7854, 58:27.

————. "The Discourse on Loving-Kindness (continued)." Recorded June 5, 1994. http://dharmaseed.org/teacher/334/talk/7855, 58:01.

————. "The Discourse on Loving-Kindness (continued)." Recorded June 6, 1994. http://dharmaseed.org/teacher/334/talk/7856, 1:09:37.

The chapter in part 2 containing the dhamma talk "Unconditional Love: Metta" from Santa Fe, NM, April 1992, was transcribed from the following talk:

Khema, Ayya. "Unconditional Love 'Metta': Loving-Kindness Meditation." Recorded January 5, 1992. http://dharmaseed.org/teacher/334/talk/7878, 1:20:04.

Ven. Ayya Khema's Metta phrases can be found in the following guided contemplation:

Khema, Ayya. "Contemplation on Loving Kindness." Recorded May 3, 1994. http://dharmaseed.org/teacher/334/talk/8006, 20:34.

The ten guided metta meditations in part 2 were transcribed from the following:

Khema, Ayya. "Most Beloved." Recorded June 29, 1996. http://dharmaseed.org/teacher/334/talk/7988, 15:09.

———. "Flower Garden." Recorded July 11, 1995. http://dharmaseed.org/teacher/334/talk/7981, 16:43.

———. "Golden Light." Recorded February 9, 1991. http://dharmaseed.org/teacher/334/talk/7968, 11:31.

———. "Sun in Your Heart." Recorded July 11, 1995. http://dharmaseed.org/teacher/334/talk/7991, 17:12.

————. "Fountain of Love." Recorded July 8, 1996. http://dharmaseed.org/teacher/334/talk/7983, 15:06.

————. "Love and Peace." Recorded January 22, 1991. http://dharmaseed.org/teacher/334/talk/7972, 15:37.

————. "Forgiveness." Recorded July 11, 1995. http://dharmaseed.org/teacher/334/talk/7982, 17:19.

————. "Seed of Enlightenment." Recorded July 8, 1996. http://dharmaseed.org/teacher/334/talk/7989, 14:48.

More guided metta meditations and other talks by Ven. Ayya Khema can be found at http://dharmaseed.org/teacher/334 or, for a more user-friendly index, at http://leighb.com/ayyakhemadharmaseed.htm.

The guided metta meditations can most easily be accessed via http://leighb.com/ayyakhemadharmaseed.htm#38.

About the Author

Ayya Khema was born in Berlin in 1923 to Jewish parents. In 1938 she escaped from Germany with a transport of two hundred other children and was taken to Scotland. Her parents went to China, and two years later, Ayya Khema joined them in Shanghai. In 1944, however, the family was put into a Japanese concentration camp and it was there that her father died.

Four years after the American liberation of the camp, Ayya Khema was able to emigrate to the United States, where she married and had a son and daughter. Between 1960 and 1964 she traveled with her husband and son throughout Asia, including the Himalayan countries, and it was at this time that she learned meditation. Ten years later she began to teach meditation herself throughout Europe, America, and Australia. Her experiences led her to become ordained as a Buddhist nun in Sri Lanka in 1979, when she was given the name of "Khema," meaning safety and security ("Ayya" means "Sister").

She established Wat Buddha Dhamma, a forest monastery in the Theravada tradition, near Sydney, Australia, in 1978. In Colombo she set up the International Buddhist Women's Center as a training center for Sri Lankan nuns, and Parappuduwa Nuns' Island for women who want to practice intensively or ordain as nuns. She was the spiritual director of Buddha-Haus in Germany, established in 1989 under her auspices. In 1997 she also founded Metta Vihara, a thriving monastery not far from Buddha-Haus.

In 1987 she coordinated the first international conference of Buddhist nuns in the history of Buddhism, which resulted in the creation of Sakyadhita, a worldwide Buddhist women's organization. His Holiness the Dalai Lama was the keynote speaker at the conference. In May 1987, as an invited lecturer, Ayya Khema was the first Buddhist nun ever to have addressed the United Nations in New York.

She wrote over two dozen books on meditation and the Buddha's teaching in English and German. In 1988, her book *Being Nobody, Going Nowhere* received the Christmas Humphreys Memorial Award. Her other English-language books include *When the Iron Eagle Flies*, *Who Is My Self*, *Be an Island*, *Visible Here and Now*, and *Come and See for Yourself: The Buddhist Path to Happiness*. Her autobiography, *I Give You My Life*, is a wonderful adventure story sprinkled with nuggets of spiritual wisdom.

Ayya Khema passed away on November 2, 1997, at home at Buddha-Haus, in Germany. Buddha-Haus continues to teach retreats in German in Ayya Khema's tradition. Please visit their website at http://www.buddha-haus.de/. You can e-mail Buddha-Haus at info@buddha-haus.de.